Confessions of a Dream Chaser

by SHARON K. SOBOTTA

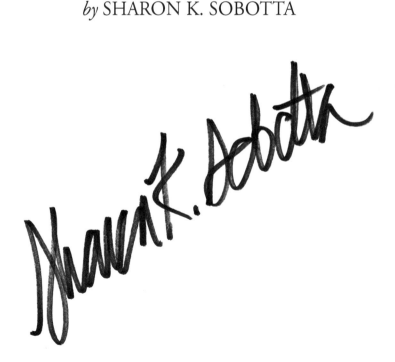

This book is dedicated to my mom for
empowering me to dream big.

Contents

Introduction

When I was ten and my sister was seven, we lay in the snow in front of our Wisconsin home, bundled up in our matching blue snow pants, our gray-and-pink moonboots, and our puffy pink jackets making snow angels and discussing our dreams. Everything seemed possible at that age.

My little sister aspired to become a Care Bear. I was pretty sure I would be the next Oprah Winfrey. I had developed a fondness for the talk show personality, as my sister and I spent time with Oprah every day after school while we waited for our dad to get home from his janitor job at the local cheese factory and our mom to return from teaching fourth graders a few towns away. I adored Oprah. She was poised, she got people to open up and share their stories, and she was incredibly confident. I could think of no one better to become.

As we grew up, however, we realized that little girls from Wisconsin didn't magically turn into cartoon characters or talk show hosts. My sister ultimately became a teacher and a mother. I moved to California and became a college administrator and a freelance journalist, which was sort of like a watered-down version of my grandiose childhood dream.

On a June afternoon in 2010, more than two decades later, I got home from work just in time to catch the second half of *The Oprah Winfrey Show*. It was the final season, and Oprah was preparing to launch her own network. Just before the commercial break, Oprah caught my attention. "Do you have what it takes?" she asked. "Upload a three-minute video and tell me what you've got, what your unique idea is, and why you deserve your own television show. This is going to be a big break for one of you."

I felt like she was speaking directly to me. Had Oprah spoken these words at another point in my life, I might have done the more practical thing—nothing. But I was in the midst of what had become the most adventurous and risk-filled year of my life. I had spent the past year soul searching—letting go of old relationships and patterns to make room for new ones and reexamining my purpose in life. I had discovered a deep passion for radio reporting. The previous summer I had taken up temporary roots in Asia. I started out in Indonesia, where I studied Balinese dance, while learning to posture my body like a bird and move my eyes like a firefly, and where I dove straight into my first international radio reporting assignment. Next I landed in Malaysia, where I reunited with long-lost friends. Then I ended up in the village of Yamagata, Japan, where I came to terms with the true value of adaptability.

Most recently I had returned from my annual trip to the New York Book Expo, where I interviewed a slew of inspiring authors, musicians, and artists who used life's most challenging circumstances as inspiration to take creative risks. I had become shameless about putting myself out there. When I saw an intriguing person, regardless of stature or fame, I unapologetically asked for an interview and I rarely got turned down. I was so inspired by the on-the-spot interview opportunities that seemed to arise wherever I went—in coffee shops, on the street, and on buses, trains, and airplanes—that I began to carry my audio recorder with me at all times.

I made ends meet by holding down a job as a college women's resource center director. I advocated for women's equality and attempted to teach men and women how to engage in respectful, healthy relationships. I loved my job but felt even more alive and blissful when I was out in the world interviewing people and producing stories—something I only did as a hobby on weekends and evenings. I heard Oprah's call for pitches for her new network as an invitation for me to revisit my childhood dream.

CHAPTER ONE
Unrealized Dreams

Within an hour of hearing Oprah's call for unique show ideas, I phoned my sister and let her know that I finally was going to take a stab at my childhood dream. I knew I would have thousands of competitors and that my odds of winning were slim, but I also knew I never would forgive myself if I didn't at least try. My mantra was that when life didn't go as planned it was best to embrace it as content. I would approach the Oprah Winfrey Network audition opportunity with that same spirit.

I decided to enter in the wildcard category for a show I would call *Off the Beaten Path*. The show would lead viewers into the depths of serendipitous encounters and stories of inspiring people from all walks of life. I didn't want my three-minute audition video to be merely a talking head of me describing my idea. Instead I wanted to demonstrate the concept by producing a video with the voices and faces

I had encountered and the stories I had accumulated while veering off the beaten path.

To do this I set up my two laptop computers—one with audio files and one with video and picture files that I had collected during the past year—on the coffee table in the middle of my living room. For the next week, I sat there reviewing images and interviews, trying to select which ones to include in my three-minute video for Oprah. As I watched and listened, I felt like I was stepping into a time capsule of where I had been and what I had experienced, and couldn't help imagining where I might head next.

My world had opened up when a Kikkoman soy sauce scholarship took me out of the small town of Whitehall, Wisconsin, and transplanted me into the heart of Tokyo as a seventeen-year-old. It had opened up further when I moved to Northern Japan at the age of twenty to attend Akita National University. I had to learn how to communicate, write, shop, and study in Japanese. I lived alongside students from Malaysia, China, Cambodia, and, of course, Japan, and communicated with all of them exclusively in Japanese. I later heard someone say that to have a second language is to have a second soul, a sentiment that resonated with me. If I could learn to thrive in my second language in a completely new context, I felt I could take on anything.

Ultimately my experiences in Japan inspired me to travel the world with purpose, and as the product of a working-class family, I had no choice but to do that on a shoestring budget. I became a journalist because nothing made me feel more alive than asking questions and collecting stories, and there was nothing I was more passionate about than giving voice to people from all backgrounds.

As I mentioned, I lived by the mantra that when life didn't go as planned, it was best to embrace it as content. That mantra helped me cope with my mishaps and unrealized dreams. When Shane, the man I had imagined myself marrying, broke up with me by suggesting that we "undefine" our relationship months before my twenty-ninth birthday, I realized I wouldn't meet my blueprint plan of having a husband and a child before the age of thirty. I felt devastated at first, and then I decided to mark the time in my life by compiling a book of universally applicable lessons I had learned from interviewing inspiring people while traveling the world. I finished writing the book *The Journey of Life: 100 Lessons from around the World* just before my thirtieth birthday.

The next Christmas, while sitting and chatting with my sister in Wisconsin, drinking wine, and overeating, as we do in good Polish Catholic families during all holidays, I came up with my next plan. I would hold myself accountable and make some positive changes in my life by practicing what I preached. I decided I would start the new year by applying one lesson a day from my first book to my own life. Just before I left Wisconsin to go back to the Bay Area, it was time for me to put lesson number two, "to embrace the art of vulnerability," into action.

Lesson: Embrace the art of vulnerability as a spiritual practice

This second lesson ensued from my having interviewed Don George, the former global editor of *Lonely Planet*, a few summers earlier. I had taken a travel writing class with Don while I was writing the book and making sense of my unfulfilled life plans. Like me, Don had begun his global adventures in Japan and kept going from there. Don spoke to me about taking risks, purposely placing himself in potentially awkward situations, and almost always having it pay off. As I reread this lesson, I realized that while I always had taken creative challenges, I rarely took intimate, interpersonal risks. I half-heartedly put myself out there and tiptoed around apologetically—never honestly stating my needs or desires for fear that I might scare someone away or perhaps get rejected. Don told me in his interview that once you embrace the art of vulnerability and put that energy into the world, people around you will reciprocate and do the same thing, and the world ultimately can end up a better place.

When Shane, the man who I had been in an ambiguous, undefined relationship with for nearly three years, called and suggested that I stop in Southern California to visit him on my way back to San Francisco, I saw it as the perfect opportunity to apply the lesson. I knew I needed to close the chapter of my life that included Shane so I could start writing the next one.

I had met Shane by accident when he had wandered into my space on the dance floor at Nicky's, a small hole-in-the-wall bar on Haight Street in San Francisco. I was intrigued with everything about Shane. He had a corporate job by day but harbored some interesting geeky qualities that I found endearing. He was a member of a speech club in San Francisco. He painted and sketched for fun. He loved his family, and I came to love them too. Less than a year into our relationship, Shane got a job in Southern California, and I stayed behind in San Francisco.

On the day Shane moved, he drove a U-Haul that contained all of his belongings, and I followed him in his BMW all the way to his new home in Hollywood. My palms sweat with nervousness as I drove Shane's fancy car and digested the fact that he would soon live four hundred miles away from me. I visited him each month and looked forward to his phone calls at the start of every morning and the end of every night. At some point Shane suggested we take a break. Then, at his suggestion, we "undefined" our relationship, which I thought was perfectly acceptable. *Who needs labels anyway?* I thought. Later, however, I realized this maneuver was just a fancy way of breaking up with me without formally letting go. We continued to speak every morning and every night and had passionate encounters each time we met. Whenever I asked where we were heading, Shane withdrew and talked about our cultural differences and how his family never would be able to accept a non-South Asian. He also talked about how much he liked the way we were. We were two people with all of the benefits of a relationship without any of the responsibilities.

"It's okay. I don't need a title," I said, not wanting to risk losing him. "I'm fine with the way things are," I tried to assure myself.

But I wasn't fine. I had put my life on hold for him. Three years later I still hadn't fully moved on.

I arrived in Los Angeles on a rainy, cold Saturday afternoon. Shane was on the phone with someone when he picked me up from the airport. It was, ironically, the woman he had been involved with during the past several months as he and I had been in sparser contact.

"You'll be okay. Cheer up, will you?" he said to the caller. "Just a minute. I'll put you on speakerphone. Say hello to my friend," he said to both of us.

"Are you kidding me? I'd better not be on speakerphone!" the woman screamed in a raspy voice.

Pleasure to make your acquaintance, I thought with a smile. *Glad I'm not meeting you in person.*

"I wanted you both to know about each other," Shane explained to me, "so I thought I would get that out of the way."

Over dinner I had the most honest discussion with Shane that I had since meeting him. Our conversation was interrupted multiple times by the other woman's text messages. She called again just before our food arrived, and Shane went outside with his phone in hand to comfort her. I ordered a second glass of wine.

For the next twenty-four hours, Shane received an influx of text messages and phone calls. He was visibly squirmy and uncomfortable. He went on to explain his relationship with this woman and an assortment of other women he had dated over the past years of our undefined time together. He explained that when men were as successful as he was, women wanted to be with them. Shane was no longer the quirky, sweet guy I had met years earlier. This was all I needed to know to let go.

Over the course of the next day, between phone calls and text messages from the other woman, Shane and I chatted, laughed, watched movies, and reminisced about the past, as we leaned against each other on his L-shaped couch with our feet resting on the coffee table that we had picked out together. When I glanced up, I saw elements of me everywhere in the things I had given him: two Japanese ceramic teapots I had purchased from the Asakasa market in

Japan, a statue of a man smoking hookah that I had picked up for him in Uganda, sketchpads with little notes from me, and the book that I was inspired, by the uncertainty of our relationship, to write a year earlier. I took mental pictures of all of it and cherished the moment I was in, as I knew this would need to be the last night I would ever spend with Shane. I knew that tomorrow when I boarded my plane back to San Francisco, there would be no turning back.

The next day we went to the last movie we would ever see together. I was half focused on the movie and half focused on what I would say to Shane before I left. The comfort of his hand on mine reminded me how hard it would be to let go of him. In my head I practiced what I would say. I wanted him to know the profound impact he had on me, that the unrealized dreams I had for the two of us had amounted to amazing content for my life story, that while having him in my life I had become the person I always wanted to be—confident, assured, and determined. I wanted him to know I had been overly patient with him, not because I was desperate but because I believed in him and thought he was less invincible than he claimed to be and because I had never experienced that type of compatibility with another human being. I wanted him to know that the reason I could walk away wasn't because I had stopped loving him, but because I had done everything I could in our relationship and it was simply time for me to move on. I knew that it was not our cultural differences that would keep us apart, since I was very close to his family and because his other girlfriend, who is now his wife, was a blonde American just like me. I knew that he likely spared me from the truth—that I wasn't the right person for him or that I was his backup plan—because he didn't want to hurt my feelings.

When we got back to Shane's LA apartment, I uttered his least favorite sentence.

"Shane, I have to talk to you," I said.

He went to have a cigarette on his balcony, and afterward we retreated to the L-shaped couch. I froze at first. I asked him to forgive me for not looking at him. I didn't want to cry. Then, in half sentences, tons of pauses, and tears I could no longer hold back, I sloppily told him. I looked straight ahead as I tightly held on to a pillow and talked through my ugly cry. I was embarrassed, but I knew in my heart that I hadn't yet taken the risk of being vulnerable and exposing my true self, as I promised myself I would. Naturally I forgot half of what I was going to say and inserted more tangents than necessary. Shane was visibly uncomfortable to see me in my ugly cry state but said almost nothing. He offered me a hug and then drove me to the airport.

When I got back to my apartment late that night, I wrote out what I had planned to say in a more concise and decisive fashion. I was in tears as I wrote the e-mail, and then with the click of the "send" button, I officially closed that chapter of my life. I cried myself to sleep but knew I would be ready to start fresh and tackle the next lesson in the morning.

Lesson: Be engaged in the world in which you live.

The next morning I pulled myself out of my warm, cozy bed and met the cold, rainy Bay Area day head on. The next lesson of the day was to be engaged in the world in which we live. I headed over the winding, bumpy Rheem Boulevard to Starbucks, where the entire staff knew my order before I placed it—a tall non-fat mocha, light on the chocolate, extra hot with light whipped cream on top. I felt a combination of emotions—heartbroken, empty—not in a depleted kind of way but in a way that enabled there to be space in my core for new life experiences. I listened to the morning news on the listener-sponsored radio station KPFA as I drove my silver Scion coupe over the hill and back to the campus where I lived and worked. I heard the chilling report that an unarmed and handcuffed twenty two-year-old African-American man had been shot dead, execution style, by Bay Area Rapid Transit police officer Johannes Mehserle. After having received reports of an unruly group of men on the BART during the wee hours of New Year's Day, BART police had intervened at the Fruitvale Station, where they restrained a man named Oscar Grant. Grant was unarmed and facedown with his hands behind his back when twenty-seven-year-old Mehserle leaned over him and pulled the trigger. Soon after, Oscar Grant was pronounced dead. Yet another African-American man had lost his life prematurely in Oakland, California.

On this particular day, I had to figure out how to get engaged in the world in which we live. I opted to blog about the importance of contributing to a more just world by challenging injustices like the Oscar Grant incident in our everyday lives. Little did I know, a year and a half later I would be the street reporter for KPFA accompanying Oscar Grant supporters as they protested the light sentence of only two years for the officer who had shot Grant dead.

Lesson: Seek unconventional knowledge from people and real-life experiences.

For the next week, I reflected on my life as I put lessons four, five, six, and seven from my book, *The Journey of Life*, into action. It was lesson eight, however, that would ultimately change my life. This lesson was to seek unconventional knowledge from people and real-life experiences. I wrote the lesson after I interviewed my Pakistani-Canadian friend, Zain, one of the first people I'd met when I'd moved to California seven years earlier. Zain's lesson was about experiencing the world hands-on, which for him translated to dance and vocal lessons. After contemplating how to apply the lesson to my own life, I decided to apply for a radio journalism fellowship program at KPFA in Berkeley. It was impractical for a thirty-two-year-old to work full-time and also do an internship, but radio would serve as a hands-on mechanism for me to make voices of people from all walks of life audible. On top of that, the story about Oscar Grant that I had heard reported on KPFA less than a week earlier had deeply inspired me. My commitment to apply a lesson a day from my book had given me an unexpected source of motivation and a sense of accountability to make positive changes in my life. After I learned that I had been accepted into the program, I considered foregoing the opportunity. I worried that once again I might be biting off more than I could chew by adding a radio fellowship to my already busy schedule. Luckily I didn't pay that nagging voice much heed.

Three months of training later, I was a weekend reporter for KPFA and soon after began contributing to other radio networks. I still remember my very first field story. I covered a multicultural women's conference that featured Gloria Steinem. I went up to Gloria, who happens to be an icon for the women's movement, and asked for an interview. She agreed. A few reporters from Nevada City's "See Jane Do" radio show joined me, and we co-interviewed Gloria. I tripped over my tongue several times and trembled with nervousness. Gloria's response to one of my colleague's questions was my favorite.

"Gloria, tell me why you think you can accomplish anything you want to and why young women should believe the same," she said.

"Oh, I don't believe that," Gloria said. "I don't think we should tell young girls they can do that either, because we may be setting them up for disappointment. Instead we should say, 'You can try anything you would like to and you will have a great time on the journey.'"

What Gloria said resonated with me.

I fell head over heels in love with field reporting. There was nothing quite as rewarding as bringing my listeners to the heart of an antiwar peace rally, a strike, or a protest, or letting them hear the firsthand accounts of students from Richmond High who were affected by the gang rape of one of their classmates.

While field reporting, I always had my eyes on a main story to finish in time for the six p.m. airtime, but I was equally intrigued and inspired by the people I encountered by chance. Similarly, in life, it was often the people I met by chance, while pursuing other plans, who inspired me the most. Every time I interviewed someone, I felt like I discovered a new dimension of myself. And because I knew that everyone had a story to share and I never knew who I would encounter, I never went anywhere without my digital recording device.

CHAPTER TWO
The Plot to Travel

It was a year of unrest. Michael Jackson died at age fifty of a sudden cardiac arrest just days before his revitalization world tour was scheduled to begin. Farah Fawcett lost her public battle with cancer, as did Patrick Swayze. Demonstrators who disputed the results of the election died for their cause in Iran. Middle- and working-class Americans struggled to make ends meet as employers distributed rounds of pink slips. Everyone was either doing more with less or experiencing the impact of others who were doing more with fewer resources. We were all reminded that we were nothing more than tiny pieces of the universe.

That same year a recently divorced high school classmate named Joe found me and wooed me via Facebook. Joe was a tall man with ash-blond hair who looked nothing like the men I usually dated. He was a talented musician and actor who had sacrificed his dreams to get married, produce two beautiful children, and work at a factory job in Wisconsin that he resented—a far cry from the path I had chosen. Joe came to visit me a few times and called me on a daily basis, and we sort of fell into a long-distance relationship. When Joe began hinting at the idea of getting serious; I started silently questioning if he was really a match for me but decided to let the relationship run its course.

As spring gave way to summer, I felt a knot of anxiety in my stomach and a suffocating pressure in my chest. I wasn't having a heart attack or developing a stomach ulcer. Instead every fiber of my body and soul told me it was time for me to travel. My passport had expired, and with the exception of a day trip over the border to Mexico, I hadn't left the country in more than a year. Perhaps it was the reality of knowing that without a valid passport I couldn't partake in a spur-of-the-moment international trip, even if the opportunity arose that put me over the edge. I stayed in the United States for fifteen months while intentionally scheduling more time with immediate family members, distant relatives, and old friends. At work I had been running a department singlehandedly after the economic realities had resulted in a temporary hiring freeze. All of this pushed me further out of my comfort zone than any trip ever could have. I had already learned from experience that no matter how far I went I could never truly escape from myself anyway. In fact, to the contrary, the further I went away from the business of my daily life, the more I was forced to reflect on the state of my own circumstances.

I wanted to go somewhere I had never been and do something I had never done before. One evening I typed "international dance" and "July" into my Google search engine, as July was my unpaid month off work. Years earlier

I had voluntarily taken a pay cut to become an eleven-month employee. At this point in my life, time was frankly more valuable than money.

Ciudamani Dance Institute in Ubud, Bali, Indonesia, popped up. I applied for the program that very day. Several months later I found myself on a plane heading to Indonesia to study dance. On my way home from Indonesia, I would squeeze in visits to two of my favorite familiar places. I would enjoy three days in the picturesque, tea-drinking, leisurely, tropical country of Malaysia, and then I would spend a week in the village of Yamagata, Japan, with my best friend from college, Nami. I would conclude my summer travels with a weekend visit with my family in Wisconsin and then head back to my day job feeling revitalized and refreshed.

CHAPTER THREE

Twenty-Four-Hour Layover in Narita, Japan

Traveling solo as a non-tourist proved time and again to be the most enriching experience I possibly could have. Despite my pale skin and blonde hair, I often was asked if I was a resident of the place I was visiting or an expatriate worker. This was Japan, the place where I had lived for a total of more than two years, the place whose language I spoke fluently, the place I had visited more times than I could count, and the place where I felt most at home. "*Omatase itashimashita. Irashaimase*" was followed by "*Sanku you for waitingu. Werukamu,*" the Japanese greeting followed by the *katakana* English equivalent of "Thank you for waiting. Welcome." Next came "*Yokatta. Nihongo wa daijyoubu desu ne,*" which means, "Great. You speak Japanese." Both parties would breathe a sigh of relief as soon as it was established that Japanese was the language we would be speaking.

On my journey to Japan for the first leg of my flight to Indonesia, I was seated between two Chinese women, whom the flight attendants had mistaken for being Japanese. When the flight attendants approached our row, it was the Chinese women whom they initially addressed in Japanese, not me. I leaned over to the woman next to me and translated.

"She's wondering if you'd like tea or coffee, salmon, or beef," I explained.

Once in Japan I rolled my suitcase through customs, boarded my bus, and headed to Hotel Nikko, where lots of JAL (Japanese Airlines International) customers en route to other places were staying. I went straight to the convenience store and picked up a package of Onigiri rice balls stuffed with salmon, one international calling card, and a can of warm green tea. I felt like I was home again. I settled into my little room, which offered an almost twin-size bed, a *yukatta* or thin cotton robe, and slippers. I went to bed for several hours and woke up before the early rising sun at around four a.m.

Michael Jackson had died just before I had left the United States. I knew from my time in Japan that even when Michael had gone through invisible streaks in the United States, his popularity never had faded in Japan. He appeared in commercials for products such as Suzuki motorbikes and television sets. Michael's music was playing everywhere in Japan—the airport, the convenience stores in my hotel, on the street, and on nearly every television station. I turned on my favorite news channel, NHK, to see and hear more about the impact of Michael's death. Tears, memorial shrines, music, and tributes filled the airways. It was four o'clock on Sunday morning in Japan, which meant it was Saturday afternoon in the US, the day that I customarily reported for KPFA's evening news. I decided to base my first international story on the global impact of Jackson's death. I put my clothes on, stepped into my slippers, and went down to the convenience store embedded in the center of the hotel to grab an early breakfast—a soba bento, a side of seaweed salad, and another serving of warm green tea—and then began to piece my story together from the comfort of my teeny hotel room.

I sat at the desk first reviewing all the sounds that I had captured with my digital audio device, while conceptualizing how to piece it all together, then writing my script, and finally producing the piece. This was the first field story I had produced outside the studio, with the help of some free audio software that I quickly found online and downloaded.

At about one p.m. Tokyo time on Sunday, I logged on to my computer and then the radio station's website so I could hear Saturday's six p.m. newscast. I turned the volume up, hopped into my bed, wrapped myself in a thin brown blanket, and listened. When I heard the Saturday anchor, Cameron Jones, say, "KPFA's Sharon Sobotta is in Japan and sends us this report," I felt a jolt of joy surge through my body. In my day job I dedicated my life to helping women and men realize and execute healthy relationships with one another. I worked with colleagues, administrators, and students to challenge all forms of oppression, but that work was more about planting seeds and hoping for the best. There wasn't necessarily a concrete result, at least not one I could see immediately. Even if I couldn't change the world with a three-minute radio piece, I could say that I had, from start to finish, created an end product in the form of a story.

The finality of this immediate, concrete product made me fall in love with the entire process of radio reporting. I loved being out in the field interviewing people, capturing the ambient sound, and figuring out how to piece it all together to help my listeners feel like they were in the heart of the story. I enjoyed writing my script and doing my voiceover. And then the adrenaline rush that happened every week at around 5:50 p.m. while weaving my voiceover and clips together in a mad rush to meet the six p.m. deadline was exhilarating. When 5:52 hit, my pulse always beat a little faster, my palms got a little sweatier, and everything around me became completely irrelevant. At 5:59, when I uploaded the piece into the Saturday evening news file, I heaved a huge sigh of relief. When I heard my piece on the radio, I felt an overwhelming sense of accomplishment.

With a smile on my face, I drifted off to sleep that Sunday morning in the comfort of my tiny Tokyo room. I felt like I was on a trajectory toward living a dream of sustaining myself through reporting, writing, and conducting creative projects.

I got up an hour later and headed back down to the convenience store for another can of warm tea, and then I found a spot to sit, took out my laptop, and began writing about the ironies of cultural assumptions. As a blonde American woman, I showed no visible indicator that I spoke Japanese, and at first glance I imagined others to assume that I wouldn't understand them. There was nothing that could be done about this, but I wanted to write about it and process my thoughts. I paused and glanced up to gather my thoughts. I don't know why. I guess a gaze into midair or somewhere other than my keyboard seemed to connect me with the memories and visuals I needed to write about.

While I was gathering my thoughts, an elderly woman came over and joined me.

"*Konichiwa*," she said. "How long have you been in Japan?" she asked in Japanese. I was pleasantly surprised. The woman had taken for granted that I spoke Japanese and immediately launched directly into her life story. It was like we always had known each other.

"I'm almost eighty, but I've never been sick in my life. I was a schoolteacher and so was my dad," the woman told me.

She was ecstatic when I told her that my mom and sister were also schoolteachers. I closed my computer and gave her my undivided attention. Not once during the conversation did she question why I spoke Japanese; she just talked. As we chatted, two women—one in her fifties and another in her twenties—interrupted us. As it turned out, they were the daughter and granddaughter of my new friend. Apparently she had wandered away from them, and they looked relieved to have found her. She didn't apologize for getting lost. She just explained the circumstances. "*Tomodachi ni narimashita yo* (I made a friend)," she told her daughter and granddaughter with a huge smile. I asked her to take a picture with me. Pictures were great for documenting all of life's most interesting moments, and the act of picture-taking served as a great bookend to any social interaction with newfound friends. I wanted a picture with just my new friend, but there wasn't really a polite way to disinvite the others.

"Let's take one of us all together and then how would it be if we took one with just the two of us?" I gently suggested in Japanese. I still hadn't phrased it gently enough. The granddaughter asked if her mother could join in the picture.

Before I could respond, the mother and daughter began bickering.

"No, she said just the two of them. She doesn't want me in the picture," the mother told her daughter. That was true but not something I could admit to without hurting anyone's feelings.

"No, it's fine. Let's take one together," I suggested in an effort to ease the tense moment.

The daughter grabbed her mom's wrist and shoved her into the picture.

After the picture was taken, we congregated as if there had been no tense moments, exchanged business cards, offered polite bows to one another, and went our separate ways. As I walked away, I felt like the entire purpose of my twenty-four-hour layover in Japan had been encapsulated in the simple conversation with my new eighty-year-old friend. She reminded me that people of all ages in all corners of the world crave the same thing—human connection.

CHAPTER FOUR
Finding Rhythm in Ubud

I arrived at Denpasar International Airport in Bali late Sunday night. I knew someone was picking me up, but I didn't know who. I strolled through the gaggle of people waiting outside the airport and had brief conversations with a few drivers. Drivers held up signs with random names and walked toward me pointing at their signs. I shook my head and smiled, politely letting them know I was not the passenger they were searching for. Fifteen minutes later Danu approached me. "Are you Sharon?" he asked. Danu had been assigned the task of fetching all of the aspiring Balinese dancers and musicians as they arrived. In my batch there were just two of us—a musician named Lana and me. Lana was a thin, middle-aged woman with short, curly brown hair and glasses, and she carried a saxophone case.

"What made you decide to come this summer?" I asked her.

"I'm a musician," she said.

"What made you decide to come here to study music in Bali?" I asked.

"Oh, well, I'm a musician," she brusquely repeated, as if it were obvious that every musician would show up in Bali for the summer.

On the drive through the narrow, dark roads with moist, slightly cool air blowing in on us as light gamelans played on Danu's stereo, I crossed my fingers and hoped I would have better synergy with the other program participants. When we arrived at Artini Cottage, the place that would be my home for the next month, the reception staff who slept underneath the open-air office space woke up and greeted us. A man named Putu carried my luggage up to my new living quarters. When I got to my room, I saw a scattering of rose petals on the bed, a bamboo closet for my clothes, ceramic tiling, and a ceiling fan. It was perfect. I took a deep breath and said out loud, "Thank you, universe, for allowing me to be here right now."

Early Monday morning I woke to the sounds of crying kittens. Apparently a mama cat had given birth to a litter of kittens overnight, right outside my room.

I lay in bed waiting for time to pass so I could get up and have breakfast. As soon as the clock struck seven a.m., I barreled out of my room and into the outdoor dining facility, where I would have breakfast each morning with all the other program participants. Each one of them had their own distinct personality, and each had been driven to Bali by a different life circumstance. Gregory was a bald, sixty-something-year-old collector of art who returned to Bali each summer.

"Why would I go anywhere else?" he asked rhetorically while sipping his Balinese coffee.

Dina was a twenty-year-old Vietnamese-American native of San Jose, California, who spoke loudly and struck a pose—usually her forearm resting on top of her head each time a camera was near. Katrina and her husband, Geoff, were a couple from Southern California. The two spent most of their time together but jokingly called me their adopted daughter. Pam was a twenty-year-old woman who had been homeschooled and was still learning to navigate the space between childhood and adulthood. She wanted so badly to be heard and seen that she sometimes squeezed herself into the small opening that existed between people sitting beside each other on the floor, in much the same way a toddler might squeeze between her parents when she wants more attention. Dee was a transgender person and a natural performer who kept the entire group entertained with pranks and practical jokes. And the list went on.

That Monday morning at breakfast, I sat with Gregory, Katrina, and Geoff. I ordered *nasi goreng,* delicious Indonesian fried rice topped with a fried egg and spicy-sweet red samba sauce. We sat chatting casually while the various participants trickled down for breakfast. Just as it was time to leave for the Bali-Banja, the open-air dance studio, Katrina pulled me aside and wrapped me in her sarong, the mandatory attire for dancing.

At the dance site, we each took a seat on the tiled floor of the outdoor studio so we could prepare for the Balinese Hindu blessing. Each person was handed five flowers, each of which had their own special meaning and would be used for a separate aspect of the five-step ritual. While following the leader of this ceremony, we picked up each flower at the appropriate time, carefully clutching it between our index fingers with our hands in the prayer position above our heads, and then placing the flower behind our ears. We did this to the tune of temple bells and the scent of fresh incense. Then came the part I had been waiting for, the dancing.

There were eight students in my group and an assistant teacher for every two students. I had studied hula and Middle Eastern dance, which were both about control of the hips and shoulders, and Indian *bhangra*, which was all about bent knees and bouncing shoulders, but never had I attempted anything remotely similar to Balinese dance. Each pose mimicked a bird. Our eyes even had a particular pattern they needed to follow. I struggled to keep my arms bent in proper position while leaning my upper torso to one side, putting my weight on the other side, and then switching. On top of that, my posture was horrible.

"Sharon, you have a beautiful head. Hold it up high and proud as if there is a rope attached to the top of your skull pulling you up toward the heavens," Judy, the program coordinator, whispered in my ear.

While that all sounded really nice, on a practical level I had no idea what it meant.

"Okay, thank you," I said. I opted just to keep watching and attempting to imitate what my instructors were doing.

Surely, there would be some way for me to catch on, and little by little, day by day, I did. The head dance instructor, Em, who was Judy's daughter, was an intriguing woman. She was born to a Japanese-American mother and an Indonesian father. Em had fallen in love with a Balinese man named Dewa, and the two of them split their time between the US and Indonesia while raising their two multicultural children. I hadn't yet decided on the topics of the weekly radio reports that I would be filing from the village, but I knew I needed to interview Em about her take on life in Bali, as both an artist and the parent of bicultural and bi-national children. One day after class, Em sat with me on the floor of her studio and gave me the scoop on her life in Bali.

"I think the idea that getting along or creating some kind of harmony is something that we have to work toward, and it is important. It's not something that we can take for granted and it won't happen without us doing something about it," she said. "I like that everyday people in Bali do something small to acknowledge that they are part of a world that's not just about human beings and not just about the self, but about a bigger world. We need to do a little bit every day for the bigger world to help create harmony," she graciously explained.

As I learned during my interview with Em, my time in Indonesia would coincide directly with the country's 2009 elections. Had I realized this before my arrival, I would have been more prepared. But I was here now, so it was my time to figure it out and begin reporting.

I was determined to collect a range of perspectives for my radio pieces. Putu, the man who had checked me into my room and frequently staffed the receptionist desk, introduced me to Arga, a woman who worked a half-block down the road from the Artini Cottage at a high-end Japanese spa strategically placed directly in the middle of the rice paddies. For the equivalent of seven US dollars, you could get a massage pretty much anywhere in Ubud; for a high-end local massage with trained professionals, you might pay fifteen dollars. At this spa, prices began at one hundred dollars, which was slightly higher than the monthly salaries of most spa and hotel employees in the town.

Arga was a twenty-three-year-old mother and wife who was a receptionist at the spa. She wore a yellow *kebayah* and floor-length skirt, and had her hair pulled neatly into a low ponytail. She agreed to share her story and her perspective.

Arga explained that each day she commuted by motorbike from her home up in the mountains down to Ubud. She worried about the quality of roads, the lack of public transportation, and the type of education her then one-year-old son would someday be able to receive. Arga shared her love/hate relationship with the tourism industry. On the one hand, the tourism industry had given her a job. On the other hand, she explained, local vendors no longer priced their items for local customers, whose wages averaged the equivalent of seventy to one hundred US dollars per month, because they knew they could get higher profits by selling to tourists. Tourism was driving up the prices of local products and services, and Arga said that making ends meet was challenging.

In the middle of the interview, she stopped to greet a Japanese couple, "*Irashaimase*," she said, which meant "welcome" in Japanese.

I was excited that Arga spoke Japanese and thought it may be easier to converse in Japanese rather than English, so I immediately switched. "Oh, no. I only know how to say welcome and thank you," she explained.

Arga invited me to accompany her to her village on election day, and I accepted the invitation. On the morning of the elections, Arga arrived on her motorbike to pick me up. I skipped my morning dance class and rode fifteen kilometers on the back of her motorbike, hanging on to her shirt for dear life and hoping that my helmet-less head would be all right if we were in an accident. Motorbike accidents in Bali are as normal as mosquito bites. (For anyone who's never been to Bali, its humid, moist warm air makes it a mosquito breeding ground.) As we drove into the mountains where Arga and her family lived, the warm breeze became slightly cooler. I'm not religious, but on the drive up the bumpy road, I said a silent prayer, *Dear God, please let us arrive safely. I want to live to tell about this day."* Arga wasn't a bad driver, but the roads were narrow, rough, and sometimes had holes in them. Nevertheless we arrived safely at Arga's compound.

Arga's village was green, beautiful, and incredibly humble. As we walked into her family compound, her father-in-law and brother-in-law were sitting on the ground near the entrance, busily hammering and chiseling away at craft projects, which would later be sold at Ubud market. Half a dozen children ran around the open-air compound, playing. Arga took a load of laundry out of the washing machine and scattered it onto a patch of plush green bushes to dry. Then Arga and I sat under her family gathering area, which was covered only by a slab of roof. Arga held her baby while six other children from the compound gathered behind me, peering over my shoulder to curiously watch the viewfinder of my video camera. They never had seen anything like it before.

After the interview, Arga and I walked over to the local polling station. Each village member waited for their turn and then went up the stairs, dunked their index finger in ink, and voted and signed with their fingerprint. Arga stood by my side and translated for me as I interviewed villagers one by one. By the time we had walked back to Arga's place, a vendor had set up a food stall on the gravel road. She was selling sweet black rice for the equivalent of ten cents per bag. With Arga's help I interviewed her and then bought ten bags of sweet black rice for Arga's family. We sat in the plush green compound, enjoying the rice and chatting about life while listening to the sounds of birds, chickens, and the hammering of crafts—the daily ambient noise of a village in Bali. After our snack, Arga and I headed back down the mountain to Ubud. Once again I held on for dear life and repeated my silent prayer.

I spent the rest of the day in my room at the cottage, listening to my sound clips, extracting ambient sound, and preparing a script. Several hours later I e-mailed the first version of my script to the producer at Free Speech Radio News in New York City, who had commissioned me to cover the elections. After I received a response from her, I went back to my room and did the next round of production edits and script tweaking. I sent it to her one more time before I got the green flag.

"Make these changes and go ahead and produce your story," she wrote.

By the time I had dinner and finished my final round of edits, it was getting late—the clock struck ten p.m., then eleven p.m. I asked one of the hotel reception guys to drop me off at the one and only Internet café that was open around the clock. I knew this from having filed earlier stories, but I'd never bothered to learn the address. I took it for granted that all of the guys just knew where it was. As it turned out, I was wrong. The receptionist drove me up and down every road in Ubud and stopped at three different convenience stores for directions.

By one in the morning, I arrived at the Internet café. The staff, which consisted of three people, was doing exactly what most people did at that time. They were sleeping. By the time I filed my story, it was three a.m. I stayed up for an extra hour and listened to my story go live. I woke up the Internet café staff, who were each resting their heads on keyboards at the café, and paid one of them to give me a ride back to my room on his motorbike. By five a.m. I was home in bed.

Two hours later I was eating breakfast and mentally preparing to head to the dance studio for the day. I was running on adrenaline by this point. Even though my body was exhausted and craved sleep, I reminded myself that I was in Bali. I needed to learn how to dance and seize the opportunity to report on a globally significant piece of news—the Indonesian Presidential election. I used my dance breaks to interview locals. After my dance lessons, I went back to the cottage to produce yet another story. By this point I wasn't feeling so well.

Okay, you can do this, Sharon. Just push a little longer and then you can rest, I promised myself. I frequently gave myself that pep talk during deadlines when I needed to push my body beyond its limits.

I uploaded my sound clips, wrote a script, and did a voiceover in the bathroom. For the record, the best place to do a voiceover outside of a studio is in a closet, a car, or if absolutely necessary, in a grassy area outside, definitely not a bathroom, but I didn't know that yet. I was learning as I went. As I was wrapping up my voiceover, I began to feel dizzy. I went back to the main part of my room, where my computer and sound equipment were set up on top of my dresser, and uploaded my voiceover file. As I waited for the file to upload,

I noticed the spinning ceiling fan above my head. I felt dizzy again, and black spots started to fill my vision. Seconds later I was back in the bathroom throwing up. It was a humble reminder from the universe that I was not invincible.

Soon after, I dragged myself out of my room, and walked at a snail's pace past the rice paddies and to the local internet café. This time I couldn't wait for a response from the radio station, so I sent my story to my producer at FSRN and at KPFA, along with a note. "Here's a story, just in case you can use it. I can't do additional edits today, as I'm under the weather, but I wanted you to have this." I wrote.

On that day, KPFA used my story, but FSRN passed. There was no room or time to take such things personally in either journalism or activism. Furthermore I had reached my physical limits. I went to bed, caught up on sleep, and started over the next day.

While I was in Bali dancing, fighting mosquitoes, interviewing locals, producing radio features, writing, and loving life, Joe, the guy with whom I had fallen into a complicated long-distance relationship, was at home with his two children, working through all of the messiness that accompanied the finality of his divorce. When I spoke to him, I could feel his resentment through the phone.

"You chose to travel. I didn't choose this," he said, referring to his dead-end job, his failed marriage, and his fatherly duties.

The first time he uttered those words to me, I knew in my heart that ultimately things could never work out between Joe and me. I was in Indonesia, learning how to hold and move my body like a bird, to move my eyes like a firefly, in the humid heat all day long. I was relentlessly pursuing passions, sometimes hopping on a motorbike to produce a story in the middle of the night, sometimes interviewing locals about their hopes and dreams for the Indonesian elections or their future. I was working night and day to make the voices of people in the tiny village of Ubud audible to the world as I produced my first paid international radio pieces. Joe, on the other hand, was in Wisconsin resenting me. I decided I should figure out what to do about Joe later. For now I needed to focus on myself and on living fully in the present.

CHAPTER FIVE
The Flava Lounge Artist

Around the corner from Artini Cottage was a place called Flava Lounge. After so much hard work covering the election, I needed to let my hair down and live a little. I went there with my new friend, Juanita, whom I had met while walking down the street a few days earlier. I was on a mission on the day when Juanita casually asked, "Where are you from?" She spotted me because I wore the same unique hooded sweater that she wore. We became instant friends. Juanita was just about my age and from Oakland, California. She had escaped an unhappy relationship with a chance trip through Southeast Asia.

Despite rave reviews, I had resisted going to Flava Lounge for a long time. I had assumed it would be overpriced and filled with foreigners. Once I arrived, however, I loved it. Beer cost fifty cents in US currency, and most important, a hookah cost three dollars. Flava Lounge became my new favorite late-night hangout spot. There was an eclectic assortment of expats from everywhere, live music every day, and spontaneous outbursts of dancing.

Each day I went there, I noticed a man who sort of blended into the backdrop. He had a golden-brown complexion, long black hair, and a sketchpad. Chain-smoking and sipping on an espresso, he sat in the corner of the dimly lit lounge. He was gazing at the bustling, eclectic crowd of South Africans, Australians, local Indonesians, and Americans who were dancing, smoking hookah, and drinking Bintang beer, as if he were taking mental pictures with his dark brown eyes. Then, with a soft smile etched on his face, he flung his long dark hair over his shoulder, grabbed his pencil, and vigorously began to sketch as if he were transferring the mental images onto his pad. I saw him do this every time I visited Flava Lounge. I assumed this to be his daily ritual.

Then one day, with a casual hello, the mystery behind the man in the corner came to an end. The thin man with a golden-brown complexion, rings on each finger, multiple necklaces around his neck, and a large tattoo on his arm was Japanese not Balinese. Because the locals struggled to pronounce his actual name, he had renamed himself Hummer.

"How did you end up in Bali?" I asked him.

"*Bali ni yoborareta* (I was called to Bali)," he said.

"By whom?" I asked.

"By Bali," he said.

With his comment, I knew I had found my next interviewee. We exchanged numbers and agreed to meet for an interview over the weekend.

On Saturday, there had been two suicide bombings in the Indonesian capital of Jakarta, and the village of Ubud was in a somber state. As I waited for Hummer outside the local 7-Eleven, I chatted with Wayan, a driver whom I had hired to bring a group of friends to the beach a few days earlier. He stayed in touch and frequently called me to practice his Japanese. Many of the Balinese locals learned Japanese so they could more effectively communicate with the Japanese tourists. "*Zan nen, desu ne?* (That's too bad, isn't it?)" Wayan said, while shaking his head as he looked at the newspaper article that detailed the suicide bombings.

Hummer arrived on his motorbike, so I had to cut my conversation with Wayan short. Hummer drove us to what people sometimes called "downtown" Ubud. We settled into the comfy couches on the second-floor loft of one of his favorite restaurants, where we happened to be the only customers. We ordered lunch for Hummer and a round of Bintang for both of us. Then I flipped through Hummer's sketchbook, silently contemplating how to go about getting the story of this mystery man. It was hard to see this gorgeous man as merely an interview subject, but I was determined.

"My philosophy of life is that today is a gift, tomorrow is a mystery, and yesterday was history," Hummer explained as I looked at his sketches.

I could see that he truly approached life as an art project—always on the periphery, blending into the background while documenting the human experience with his pencil and paper. As it turned out, Hummer had only recently taken up sketching and painting.

He told me he had taken up the art of making accessories and jewelry when he was fourteen years old because he had wanted to buy something that was out of his budget. "I found a belt that I fell in love with. It was amazing, but it was way too expensive," Hummer explained. "I gathered hundreds of coins and worked intensely for one week, and finally I succeeded. After my friends saw what I had made, they started asking me to make things for them, and then I started making things for everyone."

Soon after, Hummer began to advertise his jewelry and accessories in biker magazines and then started custom-designing pieces for each customer who emerged. As he talked, he pulled his one-pound, hand-carved bracelet off his wrist. It had taken him a year to design.

"A piece like this is expensive when I sell it," he said with a smile.

I listened and tried to do the math to calculate how this free-spirited man sustained himself or how he had won over his parents' support for his unique journey. Just as I was formulating my next question, a little rat ran across the wooden board that surrounded the mini Balinese shrine just above our heads. The creature stopped, looked at us, and then headed into the mini-shrine to take some of the offerings that were intended for the gods of the universe. I screamed, and then we both burst into uncontrollable laughter. The afternoon melted away. The intended hour-long interview turned into several hours, and an intended interviewee became a temporary friend of sorts. None of this would have happened without the interruption of the rat.

Staying true to our professions as artist and writer, respectively, Hummer and I always met with a specific agenda. Hummer worked on his life-size sketch, which was embarrassingly inspired by me, while I prepared my weekly radio report. I asked questions while he worked on creating his next piece of jewelry. Whenever I misplaced my notebook or my radio equipment (which happened frequently) and made fun of myself—saying things like,

"Sharon-*rashii* (that's so like me)"—Hummer would smile and say, "Yeah, but that's part of who you are and you should love that part of yourself too."

Over time I discovered that Hummer's parents had been in the United States and Canada in the 1960s, and the making of Hummer had inspired their marriage in the 1970s, suggesting that his free-spirited approach to life was perhaps embedded in his bloodline. To supplement his artist income, Hummer sold and traded antiques on the Internet.

"Art makes life more colorful. I have confidence that something that I make will be beautiful and will make someone happy," he told me. "I once had the chance to create an engagement ring. Knowing that I would make someone else happy by doing this made me so happy," he said with a smile. "Learning is the joy. After I die, my handmade work will still exist in the world."

"And what has been your key to being a successful artist?" I asked.

"I have faith in the universe. I believe in myself. I'm patient, and I've learned to enjoy the process as if I am cooking. I know that nothing is easy, but everything is possible."

Over the course of my friendship with Hummer, I finished dance class and moved from my beautiful cottage in Ubud to a dumpy hostel in Kuta to enjoy my last days in Bali. I paid the bargain price of 100,000 rupiah, or ten US dollars, for my hostel room, which didn't include blankets, towels, toilet paper, or hot water, but included infinite mosquitoes and a rooster that began crowing every day at exactly four a.m.

On my second-to-last day in Bali, Hummer and I decided to do our own thing. I gave him a few statues I had bought from a homeless woman on the street at the beginning of my trip, as I couldn't fit them into my luggage. He thanked me, bowed his head, touched his heart with his hand, kissed me on the cheek, and told me he would be back later to get the statues and see me again. For some reason I knew I would never see him again, and I never did. I almost had tricked myself into believing that Hummer was my soul mate. I learned later, however, that Hummer didn't believe love was something that should be wasted on any one person but instead shared with everyone in the world.

Although I still craved a long-term relationship, my time with Hummer affirmed that Joe in Wisconsin wasn't the man for me. As Hummer and I parted ways for the final time, I understood the phrase "Everything happens for a reason" more clearly than I ever had. If not for the rat, I might have finished my interview much more quickly, but I wouldn't have had the chance to form a friendship with someone who spoke the same languages as me, literally and figuratively, or explore the depths of serendipity. I wouldn't have been inspired to write this chapter, and someone on the other side of the world would have one less painting.

CHAPTER SIX
A Blast from the Past

I wasn't scheduled to fly to Kuala Lumpur until the next afternoon, but after bidding Hummer farewell I contemplated catching a flight that same night instead. By now I had a dampened soul from coming to terms with the fact that Hummer was forever gone, and my body itched and I felt rundown. I had acquired mosquito bites over every surface of my body while staying in the dumpy, unventilated, mosquito-infested hostile. Even though I was no longer under tight deadlines and should have, in theory, been able to rest and sleep in, the rooster that began to crow at four a.m. outside my door made that impossible. I knew that if I caught the last flight of the day to Malaysia I could at least rest in the plane without a wakeup call from a rooster or the buzzing of mosquitoes. Then again what would I do in Kuala Lumpur when I arrived at two a.m.?

Ultimately I decided to make due for one last night. I walked to the shop down the street from my dingy hostel and showed the shopkeeper my swollen, red mosquito bites. He sold me some herbal oil to treat them. On my way back, a man offered to sell me a newspaper for 45,000 rupiah (four US dollars). After having spent the past month in Bali, I knew the real price was six thousand rupiah. I told him I would buy a paper for that price. "Okay. Last price is 25,000 rupiah," he said, still trying to figure out how to make a profit. I looked him in the eye and smiled. Although I could have purchased a paper at market value in the convenience store, I knew this man's livelihood depended on the sale of his newspapers. "Okay, seven thousand rupiah. Then I get a little commission," he admitted. I smiled again and completed the transaction.

That night I covered my mosquito bites with herbal oil, put my beach mat on my bed, and strategically draped sarongs and other thin layers of clothing over my entire body (including my face) to help protect me from more bites. When the rooster crowed before the sun rose, I got up and packed in preparation for my next adventure. Then I took my final walk to the beach. I sat in an open-air *warung*, enjoying my final serving of Indonesian *nasi goreng* (fried rice with a fried egg on top), as I listened to the sounds of sizzling food, combined with whistles and the engines of motorbikes, horns, cars, and voices. All of this mingled with the sights of the blue-gray ocean and the eclectic mix of tourists and locals. I breathed it all in, and I felt thankful for the opportunity to have awakened in this vivid country one more day. On my way to my last breakfast there, I took a mental photograph of the sign that sat out in front of the Hard Rock Café. Emblazoned across it were the words:

THE LOVE YOU TAKE IS EQUAL TO THE LOVE YOU MAKE. This perfectly summed up my time in Bali.

Hours before I was due to depart for Kuala Lumpur, I bought an oversize duffel bag from a shop outside my hostel and shoved all of the items I had accumulated into it. I slowly walked down the street with my backpack and duffel bag and hailed a cab.

On the drive to the airport, I realized I really was coming down with something. I had the chills, my throat was starting to hurt, I felt clammy, and I struggled to muffle my cough. This was during the peak of the H1N1 swine flu scare and definitely not a good time to be sick. All the same, I was pretty sure I had acquired a good old-fashioned cold from prolonged sleep deprivation and my having pushed my body beyond its limits.

It had been years since I had been to Kuala Lumpur, and I had no plan lined up for where to go and where to stay once I landed. If I were a planner, I might have used the Wi-Fi in the airplane to figure out where I would rest my head that night or post a note on Facebook to my friends who lived in Kuala Lumpur. Instead I used my plane ride to digest what I had experienced in Indonesia. I felt like I had to make sense of that before I could take on another country and another set of experiences. I took out my journal and began writing. Here is what I came up with.

Bali is the place where I learned to walk again—first, in dance classes in Ubud, where I held my body in positions that I didn't know were possible while my teachers patiently counted satu, dua, tiga (one, two, three) and instructed me on how and when to shift my weight, hold my arms, and maintain my posture; and second, in my daily walks around the city of Ubud, where I dodged huge holes in the sidewalk and shared the narrow roads with cars and motorbikes without getting hit.

For me, Bali is long nights at the temple participating in Hindu ceremonies and then dancing as an offering to the universe. Bali is a driver named Wayan, a Japanese hippie artist who renamed himself Hummer, a bike seller named Putu who quietly sat at Flava Lounge every day until I asked him to join our table. Bali is a twenty-three-year-old woman named Arga who befriended me after I interviewed her; took me to her village to meet her husband, child, and extended family; and later discussed with me the universal mystery of relationships. Bali is sleepless nights spent covering the elections, motorbike rides in the middle of the night, mosquitoes, oceans, temples, gamelans, and hookahs. It's the place where karma comes to life and a place where you are reminded that the love you take is equal to the love you make.

By the time my plane landed at Kuala Lumpur International Airport, I couldn't mask my sneezes anymore. The temperature outside was one hundred degrees, and the humidity level was almost 100 percent. My clothes were wet and sticky, but I had the chills. I was sick! To add to my anxiety, all around me I saw warning signs about the swine flu.

God, please don't let me have the swine flu, I said to myself.

All I wanted to do was get some *teh terik*, the delicious Malaysian libation that is a mixture of condensed milk and black tea, and enjoy a hot meal. Then I would settle into my bed and recuperate. I hadn't yet figured out where I was going to sleep, so my plan was to withdraw some money from an ATM and head into central Kuala Lumpur via train and figure it out.

I breathed a sigh of relief as soon as I spotted an ATM in the airport and inserted my Bank of America debit card.

My debit card was and is my only access to my funds. I didn't carry around a credit card to ensure that I never spent money that I didn't have. Also, in the chaos of life, I didn't want to forget to pay my bill and get saddled with a huge amount of interest. Most of the time, this served me well. Not on this particular day, though. When I inserted my card, instead of being asked how much money I would like to withdraw, I got the dreaded screen telling me my service was temporarily blocked and that I should call my bank. This had happened to me before when I was in London, and another time in Tokyo, but it had never happened before I was even out of the airport or at a time when I was completely alone. One hour passed, then two, then three. I was starving and dying of thirst, but I wasn't about to ask a stranger to spare me some change. Still, I feared that I was running out of options. I called my mom collect, and she got in touch with the bank on my behalf. Finally, just before ten p.m., the bank unfroze my account, allowing me to withdraw funds and catch a train to central KL so I could figure out where to sleep that night.

I ended up at another humble hostel, just a half-step better the one I had stayed at the night before in Kuta. I had my own eight-by-eight red room with a view of the dumpsters, rats, and all the pleasantries that come along with a back alley. It was about ninety-eight degrees outside, and there was no ventilation in my box-size room, which prompted me to resort to the air conditioner. By morning I was sneezing and coughing even more. I got out of bed, gathered my things, and headed to a stall for breakfast and then down to the market to pick up a shiny new pair of shoes to wear on the next phase of my journey, as well as a new Sim card so I could have a local phone number. I had factored Malaysia into my travel plans so I could reunite with old friends with whom I had studied in St. Cloud, Minnesota, and in Akita, Japan, but I hadn't gotten around to contacting any of them yet.

As soon as I had my new phone number, I found an outdoor café with Wi-Fi and posted a note on my Facebook page. "Dear Kuala Lumpur friends, I'm in your city. Please give me a call at xxx-xxxx if you have time to meet up." Thank God for social media. On my first morning there, an ex-boyfriend, Ado, who had studied with me in Japan, called. Years earlier we had met while attending college at Akita National University. I parted with Ado because he was embarrassed about what people would think of him as a Muslim Malay who was dating a blonde American woman. When he worked through that issue and inquired about starting up a long-distance relationship years later, I already had moved on. Still, there was something refreshing about becoming friends with him later in life. I agreed to meet Ado and his wife, as well as their daughter. I really hoped they could all meet me in Kuala Lumpur, but Ado explained that he didn't feel comfortable driving in the city and it would be better for him if I just went to Putrajaya.

I've already traveled from California to Indonesia to Kuala Lumpur, I thought somewhat bitterly. *Of course it would be most practical for me to grab my suitcase and oversize duffel bag and navigate through the city to central Kuala Lumpur Station, figure out the train, and come to you all the way in Putrajaya.*

Despite my misgivings that afternoon I did just that. I was wearing a white tank top underneath my black cotton *kurta*, along with a pair of jeans and my new shiny silver shoes. My drag-along suitcase and my huge bag, which swung directly into my hip and thigh, caused me to walk at a snail's pace on my way there. I had no idea where Putrajaya was or how I would get there, but I knew somehow I would find my way. Stuff always seemed to work out eventually. When I got to Central Station and crossed the intersection to find my next train, a twenty-something Punjabi expat worker wearing a white T-shirt and jeans ran to catch up to me.

"Can I please help you?" he asked. "I feel better if I help you," he explained in broken English.

Yeah, me too, I thought. "Okay. Thank you so much," I told him.

When you travel solo, you sometimes need to rely on the kindness of strangers, although it's important to do so with caution. You stay in public areas, where you're surrounded by people, and you follow your intuition. My intuition is embedded in my stomach. If something doesn't feel right, it isn't. I'm a laidback person, and if I feel butterflies of anxiety flying around or if I find myself in the company of someone who's giving me a speech about trusting him, my intuition usually tells me to find a creative exit strategy. If not, I remain friendly, aware, and alert.

My new friend was on a budget, so he used local buses, which were cheaper than trains. When I told him where I was heading, he led me straight to the bus stop rather than the train station. Just as we were walking down the steps from the freeway overpass, I heard someone shout my name. "Sharon, is that you?" someone screamed. "What are you doing in Malaysia?"

Startled, I paused and looked around in a state of confusion. It was a classmate of mine named Rachel from St. Cloud State University. Rachel was originally from Kuala Lumpur but now resided in Kansas City, Missouri.

I hadn't seen her since we'd graduated from college almost a decade earlier. Although we didn't have much time to connect, Rachel and I took a photo together before going our separate ways. By this point my face was beet red, and I was sweating through all of my clothes.

I arrived in Putrajaya soaking wet and took a cab to my hotel. To my pleasant surprise, this place was complete bliss compared to anywhere I had stayed all summer. I had an India-themed room, complete with a porcelain bathtub, mosquito-free sleeping quarters with a beautiful queen-size bed, Egyptian cotton sheets, and a clean comforter. I washed my hair in the luxurious multi-head shower and then sat in the clean bathtub. I put on a fresh outfit and felt like a brand new person.

Slightly ahead of schedule, I arrived at the local mall where Ado's family had asked me to meet them, which gave me time to shop a little bit. Just before eight p.m., I spotted a woman who was wearing a red-and-black hijab and holding a small child. She stood beside a man who appeared to be a plumper version of Ado. Ado went to find a table and sent his wife and me inside to the café court to pick up dinner. His wife spoke little English, and I spoke almost no Malay, so the two of us just smiled and waited for the food in silence. After retrieving the food, we joined Ado at the table. During our years in Japan, Ado and I had communicated almost entirely in Japanese with a splash of English. This time we sat at the table speaking a mix of both English and Japanese and reminisced about the past.

After dinner the family dropped me off at my hotel, and I settled into my newfound bliss, expecting not to see them again. Ado, however, returned the next day with lunch— fried rice, fish, and my favorite sweet, icy dessert. I suggested that we eat in the lobby, but he said we should dine in my room so no one would see him eating with me, a blonde woman. He explained that the prospect of his being spotted with someone who looked like me made him feel *hazukashi*, shy or embarrassed.

Some things never change, I thought disappointedly. Frankly I was more worried about what people would think of a married Muslim Malay man hanging out in my hotel room.

After eating lunch, Ado went back to work, and I headed back to Kuala Lumpur. While en route from Putrajaya, I got a call from Alicia, my old broadcast journalism news partner at St. Cloud State. Alicia was Chinese-Malaysian. She had lived in New York City for years before the economic recession in the US had resulted in cutbacks in her company, prompting her to move back to her native country. Like me, Alicia was fully engaged in the process of dating, living, and learning. She was, for now, unapologetically single.

She had seen my post on Facebook and called to invite me to join her and her friends for a night on the town. I checked into my hotel, changed my clothes, splashed some cold water on my face, and had the customary pep talk with myself. I was feeling feverish and rundown, but I didn't have time to be sick.

You can do this, Sharon, I told myself, convincing myself to go out rather than rest and recuperate in my hotel room. *When is the next time you're going to be in Malaysia?*

With that I put on a pair of three-quarter-length shorts, an orange-and-blue plaid dress I'd found in the mall while waiting for Ado and his family the day before, and my new shiny shoes I'd purchased off the street, and I was on my way. If I could look good, maybe I could convince myself to feel good. I got off the train just a few miles from the restaurant where I would meet Alicia and her friends. Before meeting them I stopped at the pharmacy in the mall and consulted with the pharmacists. They hooked me up with the strongest natural herbal medicine they were allowed to administer without a prescription, and I bought a dozen packets. Fortunately the medicine offered me enough relief to spend some quality time with Alicia and company.

On my last day in Malaysia, Ado insisted that I have dinner with his family and allow them to drop me off at the airport. Ado's family had been at a picnic with friends and relatives that day, and he had me meet them at a train station because he was afraid of driving in the capital city. I packed my belongings and headed to the station once again. I ended up at the remote station where Ado had requested me to meet him and patiently waited as the shopkeepers watched me, perhaps trying to calculate how or why I ended up at this particular spot. Thirty minutes later, Ado and his family arrived. Once we got to his home, he dropped off his wife, his child, and me and then left.

For the next two hours, Ado's wife, baby, and I sat looking at each other and flipping through wedding albums, each of us anxiously awaiting Ado's return home. While we were waiting, my old friend Stanley, who is Chinese-Malaysian and also studied with me at SCSU, called and shared stories about his job, his love life, and his hopes for the future, alternately listening to my own stories. I was grateful for the call, as it helped pass the time that I was spending with my ex-boyfriend's current wife. While I appreciated her and the positive influence she obviously exerted over Ado, it seemed like a common enough rule that ex-girlfriends and current wives who don't even speak a common language aren't meant to be left together unaccompanied.

Another two hours passed before Ado returned home from fixing his car. He said he was ready to take me to the airport. When we arrived at the airport, I got out of the car and casually shook Ado's hand, as if we were business acquaintances, while his sister-in-law watched from inside.

"I want to give you a goodbye hug, but I can't," he said. "Just shake my hand."

With that I bade Ado and Malaysia farewell. As I walked into KL International Airport to catch my flight to Tokyo, I felt a knot in my throat and tears about to form in the corners of my eyes. I wasn't sad to be leaving Ado behind or sad that he had a wife and a child. Somehow the entire experience of seeing Ado caused me to re-experience the feelings I'd had when I'd broken up with him years earlier—the pain of knowing that he felt he had to hide me for fear of what others would think. It had taken me years to learn to love myself, and I definitely didn't want to travel backward to be around people who knowingly or unknowingly made me feel "less than." As I boarded my plane to Japan, I realized that my take-away lesson from Malaysia was simply that no matter how much time passes some things and some people never change.

CHAPTER SEVEN
Coming Full Circle

As my plane took off from Kuala Lumpur, I felt so sick and exhausted that I sort of wished I were on my way back to the United States instead of Japan. But my flight back home was scheduled to depart the following week out of Japan. I muffled my sneezes with my blanket and took another dose of the herbal supplements I'd picked up at the drugstore in Kuala Lumpur. I took my supplements like clockwork every four hours, as I was determined to get well and make the most of the final days of my adventure. When traveling through Japan, I almost always started out in the Tokyo suburb of Saitama where my very first host family resided. This time I would skip my usual stop and go straight to a village in Yamagata, where one of my dearest friends, Nami, resided with her new husband.

Nami and I had connected when I had studied at her school, Akita National University in Northern Japan, and again when she had studied at my school in St. Cloud, Minnesota, the following year. We were in the same international club in Japan and the same dance group in the United States. We deepened our friendship as we met to discuss the universal topics of travel, hopes, dreams, and love while trying various types of cuisines and teas.

A few years earlier, I had traveled to Japan with Shane to attend Nami's first wedding. Nami empathized with my situation—being in a relationship with a commitment-phobe—as she learned during her honeymoon that her first husband had the same issues. Two years later, when Nami married a man who was a much better match for her, I wasn't able to make it to her wedding. Now I was excited to catch up with Nami, in person, about all of the life changes she had experienced since her divorce, and to meet the man who was much better suited to my friend's gentle temperament. Like Nami, her husband was also an English teacher. I had agreed to attend school along with Nami and be her assistant teacher for the week. I always preferred to immerse myself into the culture of the place I was in and engage in the same activities as the people I was with, rather than being a traditional tourist. In addition, after having spent so many of my previous visits to Japan in urban settings, I was excited to see the dynamics of Nami's rural village school.

As soon as I went through customs and got my passport stamped, I went straight to the swine flu clearance station.

"I'm pretty sure I just have a cold, but I want to be on the safe side, so I decided to check in with you," I explained in Japanese to the middle-aged male doctor's assistant.

The man checked my temperature, went over a list of symptoms with me, and cleared me. "I'm sure you don't feel good, but you don't have a fever, so it looks like it's just a cold. *Odaiji ni shite kudasai* (please take good care of yourself)," he kindly explained in Japanese. I thanked him and silently cheered. I would not have to be quarantined after all! I got through customs, picked up a new cell phone from the rental phone shop, bought a bullet train ticket, and caught the next train to Tokyo Central Station.

If you've never made it to Tokyo Central Station during rush hour, just know that it's a place that the word "pandemonium" was made for. People run in every direction to make their connections, a "push man" stands in front of the trains and pushes people into the train cars as if they were cans of sardines, and the entire place is one big adrenaline rush. As I stepped into the familiar madness, I took a deep breath. I knew I had two minutes to figure out which direction I needed to go, locate my *shinkansen* (the Japanese equivalent of a high-speed bullet train), and board. Everything had to be perfectly timed. I clipped through at a good pace, pulling my suitcase along and doing my best to dodge the oncoming gaggle of people but bopping into a few of them with my large bag as I sped by. No one takes these things personally in Tokyo. Nobody has time to. I got to my platform as the train rolled up and breathed a sigh of relief. *Success*, I said to myself. *Yamagata, here I come!*

I took my seat and watched Tokyo speed by, watched the overcrowded streets loaded with billboards that advertised everything from Pacheko (a type of Japanese lottery) to Love Hotels (places where young couples or sometimes married men and their mistresses go to engage in extracurricular activities) give way to sparser-populated villages and rice fields. As I stared out the window at the changing scenery, my earlier doubts about whether or not stopping in Japan was the right decision quickly melted away. I knew this was exactly where I needed to be and exactly how I needed to end my trip.

When I arrived at Tendou Station, it was rainy and cool outside. I had been in the same clothes for a solid twenty-four hours. I found a bathroom inside the small department store that was connected to the station and crammed my huge bag, small suitcase, and myself in there. When I saw my reflection in the mirror, I looked and felt like a homeless hippie from San Francisco. I washed up as best as I could with paper towels and slipped into one of the dresses I had bought at the market in Indonesia and came out feeling refreshed and ready to face Japan. By that time, Nami and our mutual friend, who was also named Nami, were waiting outside the station in Nami's little white car. The three of us headed directly to a cake shop to pick out three slices of cake. We always seemed to catch up on life while indulging in delicious sweets and tea.

In the United States, dessert might be something that we occasionally enjoy at the end of a meal or without putting much thought into it, but in Japan eating store-bought and carefully selected individual pieces of cake with mini utensils is an important activity—one best paired with chatting about dreams and hopes while sipping tea. Two years earlier, when the two Namis had visited me in California, we sat around the table in my living room doing exactly the same thing. There was always something spirited and beautiful about connecting with old friends and discussing past experiences in a language other than my native one.

After we finished our cake, Nami and I brought the Tokyo-bound Nami to the train station. We rushed up the steps to the platform, watched her board, and then stood waving and smiling for a solid two minutes until she was completely out of sight. (It's an unwritten rule that when sending someone off in Japan you wave continuously with a smile plastered on your face until they have vanished.)

As soon as Tokyo-bound Nami's train was out of sight, Nami and I headed back to her apartment, changed into dresses for the evening, and headed to a curry shop to meet up with her husband for dinner. As we devoured our curry, I watched the chemistry and connection between Nami and her new husband, Kensukei. The two of them were clearly on the same team and offered support for each other as they discussed their students and exchanged stories and work advice. After a series of dating mishaps, I had started to question whether or not marriage or a long-term relationship would be feasible for me. Watching the two of them interact restored hope that I would in time find the right man to settle down with. The idea of having a teammate and companion to go through life's challenges and triumphs with, to grow with, and to come home to each evening suddenly seemed appealing.

For the rest of the week, I accompanied Nami to school and helped her teach English class. I coached one of her students, Saori, with recitation practice. I helped another student named Keiya write and edit his speech for the annual English speech contest. Keiya was the son of factory workers and was not necessarily assumed to be on the college track, but was the most respectful student I had ever met. I was the daughter of a factory janitor, and no one had necessarily assumed I was college bound either, so I had a soft spot in my heart for Keiya. There was another student named Mako, short for Makoto, the name of my clown-like friend from Osaka. Like my friend, Mako was a class clown.

Nami, her husband, and I found ways to make the seemingly mundane tasks of life fun and interesting. For example one night the three of us dressed up and found a Laundromat that was conveniently located next to a *nomiyasan* (a drinking and dining place) and drank, ate, and chatted as we did our laundry. We devoured grilled fish and veggies and *kompai-ed* over several rounds of Japanese beer. Every thirty minutes Nami and I ran to the Laundromat next door to check on the clothes while her husband continued to drink beer. At the end of the evening, when we had consumed plenty of alcohol, we hired someone to drive the car home. Another evening the three of us ventured over to an *onsen*, a community bath. It was liberating to strip down to nothing and go through all of the ritualized steps—first, sitting on a mini-stool while lathering yourself with soap and scrubbing every centimeter of your body clean and then dipping into each of the other tubs of varying temperatures. On this particular day, there were just two elderly Japanese women and Nami and me on the women's side. I noticed the older woman studying us, and then before long, she made her way over to us in the pool-size bathtub. She wanted to know if I was just passing through town, where I was from, and how I felt about the *onsen* experience.

Another day, Nami and I took the afternoon off from school, caught a train and then a bus, and headed to Sendai. Prior to the tsunami, Sendai was a prime hub for shopping and restaurants. Each evening after we were done having fun, we came back home and worked on editing Keiya's English speech. On the last day of school, before Nami's students went on break, I saw pride on their faces as they walked through their semester closing ceremony. Much to my delight, I learned that Keiya had won his English speech contest.

On my final day in Yamagata, Nami and I "*sabotta-ed*" work in the office and worked on our projects at the low table in Nami's *tatami*-matted living room. "*Sabotta*," the phonetic pronunciation of my last name, means "skip" in Japanese. In my college days at Akita National University, my classmates remembered my name because of that. "My first name is Sharon, like Sharon Stone. And my last name is Sobotta, as in skip class," I explained to them. I wish I could have similarly devised some type of memorization technique that would have helped me remember all of my classmates' names.

Nami and I went to a local sushi shop, for our last lunch to get the one-thousand-yen *tabehodai* (all-you-can-eat fresh sushi for ten dollars) and then visited the *takayaki* shop to purchase sweet bean-filled fish-shaped snacks for later. When we got back home around one p.m., Nami asked me what time we should enjoy our *takayaki*. We were both still stuffed with sushi but already scheduling an afternoon snack. We settled on three p.m. Nami set the timer and programmed the teapot to make us tea.

If you spend time in Japan, you'll learn that even snack times have a ritualistic and deliberate element to them. The younger version of me that spent time living in Japan as a college student sometimes struggled to make sense of this. *Why wouldn't you just eat when you're hungry, drink whenever you'd like, and be happy?* I used to wonder. But now the idea of setting aside computers and projects and busywork to simply drink tea and talk made sense to me. Rather than haphazardly drinking coffee or tea and mindlessly snacking while working, intentionally setting aside a small portion of time to stop working and be fully present and engaged in conversation while having a hot beverage and, in this case, sweet *takayaki* sounded divine.

During our final tea time for that particular visit, Nami and I chatted some more about relationships. Nami talked about the pros and cons of married life, and I talked about my intuition that I needed to let Joe go. Nami offered me some illuminating insight.

"The thing that makes you special is that you are passionate about collecting stories, interviewing people, and making the world a better place. *Kono Sharon no bun ga naku nattara* (if this portion of Sharon disappeared), it would be a sad thing for the world. I think you need someone who is going to allow you to be you, who supports you but doesn't resent you for pursuing your passions," Nami said. "*Muzukashii ka mo shiranai* (this may be difficult), but maybe Joe isn't the right person for you, Sharon. Meet him, talk to him one more time, and then see how you feel."

At five p.m. Nami and Kensukei drove me to the station so I could catch the 5:20 train. I was going to spend my final night in Japan at the Kamagawa Ryokan, a Japanese-style inn, in Asakasa. Nami, Kensukei, and I arrived at the station in the nick of time, just early enough for me to purchase my ticket, run through the gate, and find a non-assigned seat. I hadn't arrived early enough to purchase a reserved seat, so it was a first-come, first-serve opportunity. If I didn't find an open seat, I would have had to stand for four hours. Thankfully I found an empty seat. My seat was kitty-corner from a group of three thirty-something men who were happily chatting, snacking, and enjoying beer. The men laughed and chatted loudly, but I didn't mind. I felt happy to see what looked like a deep bond between three old friends. The laughing had a meditative quality as it blended into the background train noise. Just as I was about to drift off to sleep, an old man appeared and scolded the three men, insisting that if they didn't quiet down, he would punch them or kill them.

"*Urusai ya* (you're loud)!" he barked. "*Tanomu kara shizuka ni shite* (I'm asking you to be quiet.) Everyone can hear you!"

"We're sorry," one of them said.

Two minutes later, the old man returned. "*Mada urusai* (you're still loud)! If you're not quiet, I'm going to kill you. Why don't you come out here and fight me?" he yelled as he showed the men his fist. The man's face was red from all the beer he had consumed. It didn't seem possible to resolve the situation in a diplomatic or quiet manner.

A few minutes later, the old man returned for a third time. This time he was far more irate. The younger men were losing their patience with him.

"Don't worry about it," one of them said to the man.

The old man raised his hand and was ready to punch him in the face. At that moment the man sitting closest to the aisle spoke up. "*Ojisan, moshiwake aremasen.* (Uncle, there is no excuse.) We will be more mindful," he said.

He then bought the old man a can of beer and set it on the man's table space on the seatback in front of him. The old man rejected the beer and tossed it back, spilling it all over the floor. The young man then got up, wiped up the spilled beer, moved to the seat beside the old man, bought another round of beer for the two of them, and sat chatting with him for the remaining three hours of the journey. By the end of the trip to Tokyo, the grumpy old man had become friends with one of the men he had threatened to kill. I couldn't help smiling to myself as I watched this poignant moment unfold.

I braved Tokyo Central Station during rush hour one more time with my luggage that had expanded even more since I'd arrived in Japan a week earlier. Thankfully my flight out of the country wasn't leaving for another twelve hours, so I was under far less pressure than usual this time.

When I arrived in Asakasa, it was dark and rainy. Asakasa is an ancient part of Tokyo filled with shops and a temple that attracts locals and tourists alike. The Kamagawa Ryokan is a family-run inn. Each *tatami*-matted room comes with plush futon cushions and down blankets to sleep in. All of the guests await their turn for the traditional bathing room. It's one of my favorite places to go on my way into or out of Japan.

After I checked into my room, I dried off and sat sipping on hot tea while waiting for the receptionist to call and let me know when it was my turn to get into the *onsen* (community bath). Finally I went to the bathing room, locked the door behind me, and disrobed. As I sat on the small stool, pouring buckets of warm water over my head and body, I replayed the summer in my head. I remembered producing my first international story about the impact of the death of Michael Jackson (affectionately known as *Maikeru Jakuson* in Japan) from my room at Narita Hotel. I remembered performing dance, moving my eyes like fireflies in a village in Indonesia, and sleepless nights on motorbikes. I remembered chats, tea, and cake with the two Namis. I also recalled images of Nami's students' faces as they walked through their end-of-semester ceremony. After my soothing bath, I donned a robe and headed back to my room. When I tucked myself into my futon that night, I thanked the universe once again for the richness of all I had experienced.

I woke up to my final traditional Japanese breakfast—salmon, rice, *nato*, salad, yogurt, and tea. I was so hungry that I managed to eat all of it. When I left the *ryokan* after breakfast, it was rainy and cool. On my final train ride between Tokyo Central Station and Narita Airport, I reflected on my experiences in Japan. I realized I had been altogether transformed. Rather than resisting the immense amount of structure that came along with Japanese society, I had finally learned to wholeheartedly embrace the acute attention to details and the decision-making process that was deeply embedded in Japanese culture. It was precisely the same structure that always had been in place in Japan.

I thought about my experience on the train a day earlier when I had watched a thirty-year-old man treat a seemingly crazy drunk old man with utmost respect. He was simply showing the man the respect that Japanese culture always had prescribed for elders. It no longer seemed ridiculous to me to respect someone unconditionally simply because of age. And, after more than a decade of going in and out of Japan, I finally had stopped resisting these traditions and ways of life. Japan hadn't changed. I had.

CHAPTER EIGHT

Kindred Spirit

Fourteen hours and a transfer later, I arrived at the airport in Madison, Wisconsin, where Joe was waiting to pick me up. After I got into Joe's car, he leaned in to kiss me. As his head moved toward mine, all I could focus on was his new set of braces that he had gotten while I was away and his unhealthily skinny-looking body. Just before his lips got close to mine, I turned my head, and his kiss landed awkwardly on my cheek. We spent a strained night at my sister's house. Joe made conversation with my pregnant sister and my brother-in-law, perhaps contemplating how he would fit into my family. I just sat on the couch, doing my best to keep my sleep-deprived, jet-lagged eyes open, while accepting the reality that I soon would have to let Joe know that there would be no future for the two of us.

The next day Joe and I went to lunch. Over Chinese buffet, I explained that our timing wasn't right, that I wouldn't be moving back to Wisconsin as he had suggested, and that he couldn't move away from his children and come to California. Joe went through hundreds of scenarios about how he could make it work, but I suspected his eagerness came more from the fear of being alone than out of a genuine belief that we were right for each other.

"Joe, if I had to choose between your being with me or your being happy and successful in your own life, I would choose the latter," I said. "Go figure out who you are, what drives you, and we'll figure out the rest later."

"Sharon, I would be happy living in a box as long as I was with you," Joe explained.

With that, I knew Joe was not the man for me. I didn't think his sentiment was romantic or endearing—I found it sad. I was an innovative woman. I lived more than a thousand miles away from my family but worked hard to maintain strong relationships with them, to keep a roof over my head, and to pursue my passions. The idea that someone could consider complacently living in a box for the sake of being with me turned me off.

After lunch, Joe followed me to Main Street, which is lined with bohemian shops, bookstores, and a sprinkling of cafés and restaurants. I took Joe to my favorite bookstore, Kindred Spirit. On that particular day, a fortune-teller was doing animal card readings for a dollar a minute. I sat down with her at the small card table outside the shop. The fortune-teller instructed me to meditate on a question or topic as I shuffled the cards. I closed my eyes and reflected on the word "relationship." I opened my eyes twenty seconds later and pulled the bat card out of the pile.

"What was your question, dear?" she asked.

I looked into the bookstore to confirm that Joe was out of earshot, leaned in, and told her.

"Relationships," I whispered. "I think I'm in the wrong one."

"With him?" she asked as she pointed in Joe's direction. I nodded.

"You are," she said with absolute certainty. My bat animal card, she explained, revealed that I was craving change, looking to end old habits in terms of love, life, and work, and start fresh.

"You need someone who will celebrate your passions not hinder you," she said.

Next it was my turn to go into the bookstore and Joe's turn to have a reading. He chose the deer card. According to his recollection of the fortune-teller's interpretation, the deer symbolized his desire to maintain a calm, tame life. Again, not ironically, Joe's question was about relationships. The fortune-teller asked him if he was trying to tame me. He told me that before he could completely respond, she interrupted and said, "Oh, that one is not tamable."

The message was clear. I needed someone to love me for who I was, and Joe needed the same.

She encouraged him to try life completely on his own for a while and see what would happen if he wasn't in a relationship.

"See," I told him as I walked him to his car. "This is a turning point in life. Good things are going to happen."

I hugged him, gave him a peck on the cheek, and told him we'd talk soon. The finality of our situation hadn't yet sunk in for either of us.

It was close to four p.m. on Saturday, and I needed to submit a final story for my international series to KPFA in time for the six o'clock news. I sent Joe on his way and rushed back to my sister's home to get it done. This particular piece was based on an interview with Nami about Japan's slow population growth rate and its impact on current politics. Like always, I got the story in just in time.

It wasn't until my turbulent flight back to California the next day that I had time to feel sad about the end of my relationship with Joe. I realized on that flight that the universe has a way of working with us if we allow it to. We can either resist it or embrace it. While traveling doesn't allow us to escape life, it certainly promises to provide insight into the very workings of our lives. Knowing that with every end comes a new beginning, and that sometimes we have to let go of the old to make room for the new, gave me a burst of hope about what awaited me in the future.

CHAPTER NINE

The City of Inspiration

Nine months later I stepped out of JFK International Airport just before midnight on a Sunday morning. The familiar feel of humid summer air against my skin, the sight of rows and rows of taxis, and the sounds of honking horns were music to my soul and affirmed that I was in fact in New York City again for the Book Expo. New York is a city of intense rhythm, a city that never sleeps, a city that always calls me back year after year, and a city of inspiration.

Traveling solo to the Book Expo had become my annual ritual. Spending a week in the company of authors, musicians, artists, and millions of books that lined the six-block, two-story Jacob Javits Convention Center invigorated me. I usually stopped in Wisconsin on my way back to California to spend a few days with my family, as the Expo almost always coincided with Memorial Day weekend. This particular year my retired parents had arranged to meet me in New York. It had been a dream of my sixty-nine-year-old mother to attend the New York Book Expo, and we decided it was time to bring her dream to life. Back in Wisconsin my sister, who had given birth to a beautiful baby daughter months earlier, was already counting down the days to the end of the Book Expo, which was when I would visit my new niece.

I flew into New York one day ahead of my parents so that I'd have time to catch up with my old friend Alex. We had met when we were both seventeen and were forced to become friends when we had been the only two Americans placed at Urawa High School just outside of Tokyo. Although I later became fluent in Japanese, neither of us spoke the language at that time, and neither of us blended in. We lost touch for almost a decade before reuniting on Facebook. From opposite ends of the coast, Alex and I had stayed in touch, regularly swapping dating stories and advice.

Scanning for Alex, I stood in the midst of the midnight traffic in front of JFK until he pulled up in his posh little black car and honked. He then drove us to his home city of Long Island. We ended up having several rounds of drinks at a local dive bar. Finally, at four thirty a.m., I retreated to the loft-style room in Alex's apartment that his ex-girlfriend, Alissa who now lived next door, had just vacated. Two hours later I woke up to bright sunlight glistening through the window, and a pounding headache.

After eating breakfast at a nearby Greek diner, we were en route to Sparkling Point Vineyard to meet up with Alissa. In her job as a Steinway Piano sales rep, Alissa had organized a special event where a jazz pianist and singer named Jon Regan was performing. I'll admit that while I've slowly come to acquire a taste for jazz, I was much more excited about sipping Champagne with friends than I was about hearing the musician. But while sitting outside the verdant winery, having a glass of champagne, I couldn't help tuning into the music, which was ideal for the ambience. There was something distinctly charming about the songs that Jon Regan was playing and singing, and it prompted me to purchase one of his CDs. I would have been happy just to buy a CD and give it away as a gift, but the wine servers searched for a pen and insisted that I should get Jon's autograph. After Jon finished his set, I approached him.

"Who should I make it out to?" he asked.

"I don't know who I'm going to give it to yet, so just sign it," I said.

Jon gave me a look and then looked back down at the CD.

"To whoever this is going to," he wrote.

Since Jon was done playing for the day, I decided to ask him for a quick interview, and he agreed. As I came to learn, the forty-year-old musician had taken up singing only seven years earlier, when he had noticed that conventional jazz just didn't capture his experience as a man, as a hopeless romantic, or as an artist.

"It's pretty amazing to be able to capture the human experience in a three-minute song," Jon said.

"What is it that inspires the content of the songs?" I began to ask, but before I could finish the question, he responded.

"Girls," he said with a smile.

At the time I was working on a blog called "The Rhythm of Change." I asked Jon what that phrase meant to him and how it fit into his life as an artist and as a man. This question excited him.

"If there was ever a poster child for the rhythm of change, it would be me," he said. "I think that the most graceful and most profound thing you can do as an artist and as a human being is to accept and embrace change. You don't want to make the same album, have the same argument, the same life every day. If you can inject that spirit of embracing change into your life, then there is always something to be excited about. I think Al Pacino said, 'You're as good as the chances you take.' To me that is kind of the truth."

I asked Jon to tell me how his life path had led him to become a pianist and vocalist.

"I feel like I knew how to play the piano from the time I sat in front of it. I taught myself how to play and knew by the time I was a teenager that I was going to do that. I went to music school and moved to New York after I graduated and started to try and make my way as a musician. In the city I started in jazz gigs as just a piano player, getting known as a guy who wrote and played his own music. When I was thirty-two, I decided I wanted to write songs and get back into pop music," he said.

Jon explained that he had found that some jazz music had started to feel stagnant to him.

"I thought the most authentic thing I could do was to have the balls to write about what my moments are about. And I guess that is the lesson. Once you find your own story, you can fly a little bit. Since then I've made my living as my own artist-self."

I asked him to tell me about some of the steppingstones to becoming a full-time professional independent musician.

"It's tough when you're trying to find your way and put yourself on the map and working day jobs that you hate," Jon said. "I've probably had twenty-three different day

82

jobs. I worked in advertising as a secretary. I was a waiter. I worked in a cigar bar. I tested asbestos samples. I worked at Pottery Barn. I sold real estate. I did anything I could to get my piano tuned. So it was difficult. I think what has kept me on the map is that I have a big affinity for playing live. In this day and age, with record companies falling apart, it's still about getting on the road and playing. If you can build a following somehow, get people to come out to your shows, it doesn't really matter. I sold five thousand copies of my last record, and it wasn't on a label. It was because I made music and people liked it. It's definitely a constant struggle. When you work in the creative arts, you never know what is coming next, but that is what is great about it."

Jon revealed that the main lesson he had learned on his journey as a musician was to get lost in the process.

"Nothing for anybody, especially for me, ever happened in the timeline that I expected it to. By some stretches of the imagination, I'm forty and I should be looking at a sunset of my life, but my life has just begun. I've been in the music business for twenty-five years. I've been trying to have mainstream success since I was fifteen years old. I never had mainstream success, but I have had a lot of success by the fact that I'm in this business and loving every minute of it. If I were going to offer others some advice, it would be to stay open to every day, because if you're so busy trying to get somewhere you're going to miss what happens along the way. For me everything happened at least ten years later than I thought it was going to happen. Because I was doing the work all the time, it came back to me. I'd say, 'Don't stop believing,' like Journey [the rock group] says."

After I finished Jon's interview and the Champagne had worn off, Alex drove us back to Manhattan, where my parents were waiting at the Paramount Hotel. The Paramount was trendy, hip, and in the middle of Time Square, but its rooms were tiny. Our room had two beds that were just inches larger than twin-size beds. On our first night I noticed half of my mother's body hanging over the side of the bed that she shared with my father. She insisted that she was fine, but I didn't believe her. Then we both burst into uncontrollable laughter as we thought about how ridiculous our three-hundred-dollar-per-night room was. We opted to get the front desk to deliver a rollaway to ensure that no one would fall on to the floor in the middle of the night. We may have been in the heart of Times Square, but we certainly weren't comfortable. This was only the beginning of our New York City family adventures.

My parents still lived in the same tiny town where I'd grown up, Whitehall, Wisconsin, with a population of 1,500. While my mom had ventured across the world and visited me in Tokyo when I was a college student living abroad, my dad lived a fairly sheltered life. The hustle and bustle of the big city at the hands of their fly-by-the seat-of-her-pants daughter was a lot for them to deal with.

When I took my parents out, people asked me where they were from and complimented me on being a patient tour guide. Tour bus guides who stood in Times Square with clipboards watching for tourists were on the lookout for people like my parents—people who turned their heads back and forth to get their bearings, people who stopped abruptly to take a breather, people who weren't quite in sync with the rhythm of New York City. Although my mom didn't use a cane when she was at home, she carried one everywhere she went in New York and kept her eyes fixated on the ground in front of her to ensure that she wouldn't miss a step. My dad walked at a leisurely pace and stopped frequently.

"Where are we going?" he would ask. "How much farther?"

On the first day of the Book Expo, I put on my flip-flops, threw my wedge platforms into my bag, and departed for my twenty-two-block journey to the Jacob Javits Convention Center. While I was interacting with inspiring authors and publishers, my parents went for a walk. Within minutes a city tour bus guide had recruited them. When I called and checked in with them at lunchtime, my mom was having the time of her life and was excited about all the sites she was seeing, while my dad reported that he wasn't feeling well. That evening when I returned to the sixth floor of the Paramount Hotel, I heard a familiar sound as soon as I stepped out of the elevator. My dad was gagging loudly and then throwing up. He had motion sickness and would not revert to his normal self for three days.

The next morning we were ready to start fresh, or so we thought. We picked out a restaurant for breakfast with the plan to part ways for the day. I was attending the press conference, and my parents would tour the city for a second day. Just before our food arrived, I noticed my dad become pale and quiet.

"Do you need to go back to the hotel?" I asked.

"Yeah," he said. "I just don't feel good."

I quickly escorted him back to the hotel and then ran back to the restaurant where my food was waiting. After breakfast I walked my mom to the bus departure point and then dashed into a local drugstore to buy some fluids and crackers for my dad. I checked on my dad one last time and then began my daily walk across Manhattan to my press conference. I arrived minutes before it began. Phew.

At the opening press conference, I ended up sitting at the same table as Dr. Ali Benizar, who was a writer for the *Huffington Post* and the author of a book called *The Tao of Dating*. Ali was tallish, had a shiny bald head underneath his white-brimmed hat, and wore a pair of dapper, shiny, white shoes. He pronounced his name not like most Iranian-American men I knew, but in the same way that women named Alison shorten their names to Ali. By the time the press conference began, Ali had agreed to be interviewed, and we had exchanged numbers. I equated Ali to something between a godfather and a protective, older, brother-like figure, and someone to refer back to between events.

A few days later, while sitting on the balcony of a posh New York nightclub, Ali and I talked about life, love, and relationships. Relationships seem like the one thing all humans are on a lifelong quest to figure out. We are either in one and trying to figure out how to navigate, not in one and on a journey to find the right one, or mending a broken heart and trying to move on. The key, Ali said, is to love yourself first. I struggled to crack Ali's code and get the personal back story that had led him to explore relationships on such a deep level. I always had prided myself on extracting the stories that made people unique and that described how their life circumstances had led them to their current choices. I had discovered that while people often wanted to skip over the vulnerable parts of their own narrative, these were also the points of universal connectivity, which would make the interviewees' stories relevant to listeners and readers. Little by little I got a glimpse of Ali. He had served as an advisor at Harvard and noticed that many of the students he was working with struggled to figure out relationships. This inspired him to develop a text book approach to dating.

"What are some of the struggles you faced and saw in the students at Harvard?" I asked.

"I suppose you could call me a late bloomer. I had my first kiss when I was nineteen and was a virgin until very late. I really had no idea how to deal with women, or how to bring them into my life. So this was a skill set that was entirely missing. It is something that can be learned. So I looked on the Internet and found some books and some resources. Stuff started to work better, and I realized what works was diametrically opposed to what should work," Ali explained. I wanted to hear more about his personal journey that had prompted him to begin to study what he referred to as "the art of dating."

"So you waited until you were nineteen to have your first kiss?" I questioned.

"Waiting, yes. That would imply that I had some kind of choice in the matter," Ali said with a hint of sarcasm. "I didn't know what to do. I was hanging out with a woman that I liked and making no moves. Eventually she got sick and tired of it and just attacked me," he said.

Ali was anxious to stop talking about himself and to get back to the principles he had written about. "I deliberately based my book not on my own experiences but on principle," he said. "I'm not a poster boy for anything. It's like a physics professor doesn't have to jump out of a window to demonstrate gravity. You can just take my word for it. I tell people to focus on what they want. If you drive down the road telling yourself not to crash, you will crash. Focus on the destination. If you say, 'I want to have a harmonious, fulfilling relationship,' that is what you are going to have."

I asked Ali what advice he could offer to others who were in the thick of the dating game. His advice was simple but profound.

"Be the best possible version of you that you can be. If you work on yourself, if you are a good person, if you have a lot to offer in a relationship, then the world is your oyster. Be the person you want to be. The fact is, you have to start with the 'be.' Being that radiant, self-sufficient, interesting person, people just gravitate toward you. They want to be around you. Don't think, *Oh, this guy is a bad boy. I will date him for a little while and then find someone better.* No. That is like eating dessert all the time. It is a bad idea. Think about you first. The rest of the world will take care of itself."

Ali may have been talking about dating, but really his advice sounded applicable to all realms of life. Like me, Ali lived in California. For him, home was the sunny beach community of Santa Monica, an hour's plane ride and a short drive away from where I lived in the Bay Area. I didn't expect to see him again, but a month later I would bump into him in a Kohl's parking lot in Orange County. He would be part of my competition for the Oprah Winfrey Network.

Back at the hotel, my adventure with my parents—equal parts trying and illuminating—continued. I had one parent who couldn't stomach a cab ride and another who couldn't walk more than a short distance due to her weak knee and bad ankle. By now my dad had rested for a full day, my mom had seen the major sites of the city, and we were ready to take a cab to hear Barbra Streisand deliver her keynote speech at the Book Expo. We sat in the backseat of the cab with sweat dripping down our faces in the humid ninety-degree day. Because it was rush hour, we weren't getting anywhere fast. While in bumper-to-bumper traffic, my dad turned pale and then started to clear his throat and cough. I knew what was about to happen.

"Driver, can you pull over?" I asked.

My dad got out of the cab just in time to vomit into a blue plastic bag he was carrying along as a precautionary measure.

"Please drop my mom off at the Jacob Javits Convention Center on Eleventh Street," I leaned in and instructed. My dad and I then headed to the same place on foot.

It was around six p.m., and crowds of people lined the sidewalks. Some were determining where they should go for happy hour while others sat outside sipping coffee and chatting. My dad walked down the road, passing the outdoor diners, gagging at the top of his lungs, and then projectile vomiting into his plastic bag.

We were about to find out that while Barbra Streisand was a fantastic singer, speaking was not her forte. We listened to her wax poetic about home design and her multimillion-dollar mansion that families like mine didn't even dream about. After an hour we all agreed that we'd had enough of Barbra and decided to head back toward our hotel for dinner. I gave a cab driver instructions to drop my mom off at Rockefeller Center and then began a three-mile hike with my dad. My dad was traumatized at the mere thought of setting foot into a moving vehicle, and I was equally concerned.

Almost an hour later, my dad and I caught up to my mom, who was patiently leaning against a post in Rockefeller Center and waiting for us. We sat at a table in an open-air restaurant, hopeful all three of us could stomach a meal. We ordered before my dad abruptly got up from his seat. Soon after, the hostess approached our table.

"The gentleman told me his stomach wasn't feeling well. He wants you to eat, and he'll meet you afterward," she said.

Throughout the week, we had loads of experiences just like that one. I sometimes lacked the kind of patience required to tend to a mother who hobbled along and a father who was overwhelmed by the big city and its breakneck pace to the point that he was physically ill. My parents, however, ultimately allowed me to experience New York through a new set of lenses. My walks with my dad allowed me to get a glimpse of the world through his eyes. Going to the Book Expo with my mother, an avid book lover and a woman with forty years of teaching experience under her belt, allowed me to see new depths of her.

I paid attention to which authors excited my mom and made it a point to interview them. After studying the list of featured authors, my mom was most excited about Debbie Macomber. She had been reading Debbie's books for years and couldn't wait to get in line to meet her and receive a signed copy of her latest book. I tagged along and pulled Debbie aside to request an interview. I needed to see what this woman, who intrigued my mother and thousands of other people, was all about. Debbie had short brown hair, average clothing, and was perhaps the most jolly, down-to-earth person I had ever met. Talking to people like Debbie, I felt like I was connecting more deeply with my own mother.

Debbie was the author of more than a hundred books, but she didn't share such information without being prompted to do so.

"What most inspired your latest series?" I asked.

"Two house payments," Debbie said while giggling.

I pushed her a little more. She said community, relationships, and family dynamics had inspired one series.

Another series was inspired by her passion for knitting. My own mother had fallen deeply in love with knitting and even had joined a knitting club.

"I am a yarn-aholic. I need a twelve-step program for my yarn addiction. Because I've knitted since I was ten years old, I have a real love for that craft. When I combined my passions of knitting and writing, that is when my career skyrocketed," Debbie said.

We delved deeper. "What is it that led you to writing, Debbie?" I asked in anticipation of a very simple answer, but this question had a sobering effect on her. If she were an onion, the question would have peeled off her top layers. Debbie shared that while she always had wanted to be a writer, she had thought it was out of the question for her. She was dyslexic and didn't learn how to read until the fifth grade.

"I didn't dare tell anyone, not even my friends, that I wanted to be a writer because I knew the minute I did, they would trample all over that very fragile dream with all the reasons and excuses for why I shouldn't be a writer," she remembered. "When I was thirty, my cousin, that I was very close to, died of leukemia. I really felt that God was telling me that if I wanted to be a writer, the time was now. You cannot just continue to shove your dreams into the future. I had very good justifications to make excuses as to why I couldn't be a writer, but I wanted to do it anyways. I rented a typewriter, put it on the kitchen table, moved it at meal times, and that is how I started as a writer."

Debbie went on to tell me about one of her elementary school teachers who had warned her not to dream big.

"I can remember my third grade teacher telling my mother that Debbie was a nice little girl but she'll never

91

do well in school, and I didn't. I couldn't spell worth a darn, and I struggled with reading. I have a love-hate relationship with words. I use words to create stories, but I have a terrible time dealing with words. So it's kind of an oxymoron that I should be a writer."

It was true that school wasn't Debbie's thing. She graduated near the bottom of her high school class, got married as a teenager, and eventually became the mother of five children. Naively I asked her how she had overcome dyslexia. She explained that while you can't overcome dyslexia, you can learn to compensate for it.

"I had to learn to be a writer. I had to study words, I had to study English and learn novel structure, but I am a born storyteller. And those stories just throbbed within me. If you burn your hand, it throbs with pain. Every time I would think about a story or about being a writer, I would throb with joy."

Finally I asked the bookend question. "What's the most important lesson you've learned on your life journey so far?" Again her answer was raw but profound.

"We can't listen to the outside voices. We have to listen to our own hearts and not be afraid to dream big. I didn't dare let anyone tell me I couldn't do it, because I wanted it so badly. I remember praying for just one book, and I've been blessed beyond measure and beyond my expectations. Believe in yourself, believe in the power of your dreams, be passionate about it, and do not listen to the negative voices," Debbie advised.

The next author on my mom's list was a woman named Tosca. She was a lean woman with immaculately placed hair, a bright-blue fitted dress, perfect posture, and a tucked-in tummy. She had overcome issues with food and weight and written about her journey. She stood beside me, posing for cameras as she answered my questions in a rehearsed manner. During her interview, she told me that her secret to staying fit and healthy was learning to put herself first. My mom had struggled with her weight her entire life, and she was on a constant quest to get healthy. Perhaps that was what had led her to Tosca, the author of several health and weight management books.

While walking along with my mother and contemplating which author to visit next, someone handed each of us a green bag that said "Peace, Love & Veggies." I got in a line that led me to the signing station of Kris Carr, author of *Crazy Sexy Cancer Tips*. Kris was a thin, energetic blonde who happened to be living with stage four cancer. After the line of fans subsided, I interviewed Kris. She talked about her pre-cancer life, the time when she had thought she was invincible, trying to plow through life rather than listen to her body, before she had received her dramatic wakeup call. I happened to be a woman who had a multi-nodular, multi-cellular thyroid, three times larger than normal, as well as chronically enlarged lymph nodes and Hashimoto's disease. I also had a habit of running myself ragged and treating my body as if it were invincible. Kris was more than an interview subject to me; her story struck a personal chord.

After being diagnosed with stage four cancer, Kris took matters into her own hands. She moved out of the city, went back to school to study nutrition, changed her diet and lifestyle, and started a website called crazysexylife.com. As Kris described her own journey, I could see she was a fighter.

"You've really learned to be your own advocate. What advice would you offer other women about becoming advocates for themselves?" I asked.

"No one is going to give you permission to live. That permission is your birthright, and so if you can't stand up for yourself, make it your New Year's resolution starting today," she said with conviction. "When you start to make changes in your life, the energy really shifts. It brings about unexpected beauty and peace that really connects you to your spirit."

I asked Kris to tell me how her life changed after her cancer diagnosis.

"BC [before cancer] I was an actress and a photographer living in the city," she said. "I was burning the candle at both ends. I lived on fast food and prepackaged things. Anything that was 'good to go,' preferably with a martini, was perfect. When I was diagnosed and found out there was no treatment, I left the city and went on a huge journey around the country looking for different integrative modalities that might help me. I made a film about it for TLC called *Crazy Sexy Cancer*. That was the beginning of cancer really being a teacher to me," she explained.

"Cancer definitely made my life a better journey," Kris continued. "It has been my teacher. I think whenever we hit our tipping point, it is usually a sign. You can go one way or you can go another. I think I chose the right way, which was really going back to the basics and learning how to take care of myself and not be a weekend warrior about it," she said.

"I really started to live the life I said I was going to live. I moved out of the city and into Hippyville, which is also known as Woodstock," Kris jokingly explained. "I went back to school to study nutrition. I started juicing. I changed my sleeping habits and reduced my stress. The biggest problem we all have is stress. What a lot of people don't understand is what we eat also creates stress. You can increase stress by eating too much processed food or animal protein. I wasn't sure how the changes I was making would affect me or how long I'd be alive for, but I knew I had nothing to lose. What started as this journey looking for a cure turned into a journey of finding my life. So far I've been doing just remarkably, and my cancer is completely stable."

I asked Kris how she ultimately decided to take up writing.

"I probably had thirty journals under my bed from years of writing, but I didn't think I had what it took to be a writer. But after I was diagnosed with cancer and learned to deal with that, I thought being a writer should be pretty easy. I asked myself what I had to lose. Absolutely nothing!"

By the end of our five days in New York City, my parents and I had collected enough books to start a library. My mom had seen much of New York City by way of a tour bus by herself, while my dad rested in the hotel room recovering from an upset stomach. I had interviewed thirty-seven people. My parents were worn out, but I felt like I was just getting warmed up. I wanted to stay longer, delve more deeply into the human experience, and work on my next book. Staying longer would have meant foregoing my scheduled stopover in Wisconsin to spend time with my sister and my four-month-old niece. When I told my parents I was contemplating staying in New York City a little longer, they had their typical responses prepared.

"You have to do what's best for you, honey," my mom said with a sad look.

"Come home, honey," my dad encouraged.

Then my sister called my cell phone as I was dining with my parents. She put my four-month-old niece, Ava, on the phone.

"Do you want to see Auntie tomorrow, Ava?" my sister asked her daughter in a high-pitched baby voice. "Yes, you do," she said in the same voice, as if Ava had just signed the message.

"Okay, everyone," I said. "It's settled. I'm coming home tomorrow."

I packed my things and set my alarm clock for six a.m. so I could have time to grab coffee and breakfast and take one more stroll in the city before catching my flight to Wisconsin. When I walked through Rockefeller Plaza the next morning, I noticed that it was set up for a concert, and the band OneRepublic was in the midst of an early-morning rehearsal on the set of *The Today Show*. I decided to go into the gated area for a while and strategically found a spot, which happened to be right beside the band's drummer, Eddie Fisher, and his drum set. I couldn't stand so close to the drummer of OneRepublic and not ask for an interview, so I did.

Eddie was humble and took nothing for granted. In the process of pursing his dream of becoming a drummer, Eddie's marriage had ended and he had spent time living on the streets. As he put it, though, "Dreams aren't supposed to be easy to accomplish. Otherwise they wouldn't be dreams."

It was the most inspirational five-minute interview I had ever done and was the perfect way to end my week in New York. As soon as Eddie walked away, I pushed the button on my audio recorder to listen to my masterpiece, only to discover that it had not recorded. As I contemplated what to do, Eddie's words replayed in my head. I sucked up my pride and caught Eddie just before his group went live to ask if we could do a three-minute repeat of the interview after his set, and he graciously agreed. After Eddie finished playing, he autographed cds and took pictures with fans as he responded to my questions.

I asked him what had led him to become a professional drummer.

"I liked banging on things ever since I was a kid. I was always a tapper. I went to a U2 concert in 1987, and ever since then, I said I wanted to play music for a living. It took a lot of persistence, drive, and sacrifice to get to where I am. I was always like, 'I haven't eaten, but I want to play!' I was homeless for two months. I was starving. I lost a wife. It's not something I would choose to go through, but if you want to follow your dreams, sacrifice is required. Dreams don't come easy. If they were easy, they wouldn't be dreams."

I asked Eddie what practical advice he might have to offer other people who have big dreams. First he suggested that people be intentional about living within their means.

"Don't get into debt. Don't spend money on a fancy car, a house, and other non-essentials. Live simply," he advised. He believed those things could distract people from what could bring them true happiness. Then he did a little pep talk.

"If I had to offer advice, I would say be persistent and perfect your art, regardless of what it is. Don't take it for granted. Respect it. There are so many people who play music or practice their passions as a hobby. I hear a lot of people say that they'd love to do their passion as a living. The question I have is 'What's stopping you?' If you have a dream, it's up to you to follow it, because it's not going to come to you. You have to go after it."

Right when I finished Eddie's interview, I spotted Lenny, the man who had gotten up faithfully and without fail at three a.m. to travel from the Bronx to Manhattan to stand on the set of *The Today Show* every morning for the past two decades. If you watch *The Today Show* on NBC on any given day, you'll know that Lenny is the tall, thin, African-American man you are likely to spot in the crowd at Rockefeller Center. If you'd like to have your thirty seconds of television exposure, production interns recommend standing near Lenny.

When, by chance, Lenny had ended up standing near me the previous summer, I'd decided to seize the moment and get a snippet of this vibrant man who had captured the world's attention from the periphery of *The Today Show* set morning after morning. Since I'd neglected to take Lenny's picture at that time, I knew I couldn't leave New York City without finding him. I kept my eye on him, and the minute he grabbed his bag to begin his daily stroll through the city, I dashed over to him.

I caught up with Lenny, snapped his picture, and interviewed him again. A year had passed since his last interview, so perhaps he had new insight to share. As I was chatting with Lenny, about a dozen people approached him to take pictures with him and tell him how much they appreciated his daily presence on the show. Lenny posed for several photographs and graciously continued to answer my questions until security ushered us out. Lenny had a set routine. After waking before the crack of dawn each day to secure a spot on the sidelines of *The Today Show*, he walked the city, window-shopped, and sipped tea. It was the simple things in life that made Lenny tick.

"I used to watch *The Today Show* on Saturday, and my sister told me that if I ever came to New York I had to go and visit the set," he told me. "After I got here, I popped in one day and they sort of adopted me, and it's been quite nice ever since. When I'm not at *The Today Show*, I walk about and enjoy the city, and I do lots and lots of shopping, because I'm retired now so I've got lots and lots of time. I was in the military for twenty-five years, where I did a bit of everything. I lived all over the UK but was mainly in Manchester. I enjoy being in New York. My sister lives near Connecticut, so I go and join her every Sunday for dinner, and it is really nice to spend time with my nieces and nephews."

Lenny's secret to staying happy was simple: "No wife, no kids, no stress."

I squeezed in one more question, before security instructed us to vacate the set. "Lenny, people have been lining up to meet you since I started interviewing you today. How many people do you meet on a given day?"

"Oh, sometimes twelve, sometimes a few more. There's nothing special about me, but somehow people just can't forget this ugly face," Lenny poked fun of himself. "It makes me feel really happy. People say that I inspire them," he said with a bright smile.

After one more photo with Lenny, I rushed toward my hotel with an ear-to-ear smile. I called my airline to see if perhaps my flight was running behind, which would have been my only shot at making it. My flight was on time and scheduled to depart in forty-five minutes. In rush hour traffic, it would take me longer than that to get to the airport. I called my parents, who already were boarding their plane, to explain my predicament and wished them a safe journey. I went to a Starbucks with Wi-Fi and began to look for a new flight back to Wisconsin, but getting a last-minute ticket on Memorial Day weekend was next to impossible. Instead I bought a bus ticket to Baltimore, where I would go and visit my old college friend Elias and his family, and a plane ticket for two days later out of Washington, D.C., which would get me back to California just in time for work on Tuesday. (Because of Memorial Day weekend, Monday was a holiday.)

I checked into a cheaper hotel and bought a ticket for the opening night of *Sex and the City II*, which was playing across the street from where I was staying, in the same theater where a portion of the movie had been filmed. There were lots of women of all generations decked out in party attire for the premiere showing of the film and only a handful of men whom I speculated were dragged there by their significant others. The movie was set in Dubai, a city just a short plane ride from Doha, Qatar, a place I had frequented.

By the end of the film, my stomach was rumbling with hunger, and I was craving falafel after being reminded of all the delicious treats in the Middle East. I left the theater and wandered around Midtown. If there was one place where I should be able to find falafel at any hour, it was here. After wandering for less than three minutes, I wound up at a street stand owned by recent immigrants from Pakistan. The vendor had migrated from Karachi to help his brother run street food stalls and a limousine service. Most important, he hooked me up with a huge serving of falafel and rice.

On Sunday I hopped onto a bus that took me from Manhattan to Baltimore, where I would meet up with Elias, who is originally from Bangladesh, and his family. He had befriended me during my freshman year of college at St. Cloud State University. Although I had stayed in touch with Elias over the years, it had been a decade since I had seen him in person. Now he had a wife named Rebecca, a six-year-old son named Rayan, and a newborn baby named Ava. Elias and his family picked me up in Baltimore and drove me to their home in Pennsylvania. That evening Rebecca prepared a five-course Bangladeshi meal with curry, fish, veggies, and lentils, and we sat around the table chatting and eating for hours.

Elias shared that at some point he had gotten tired of the dating game and decided to get some help from his loved ones. Several years earlier, while he was living and working in Iowa, relatives had decided to introduce him to a series of potential mates. When Elias flew to Baltimore to meet Rebecca, he felt a strong connection with her from the start. Elias and Rebecca agreed to stay in touch and work toward an engagement. But Mother Nature presented him with an obstacle. At the end of the weekend, when Elias was ready to fly back to Iowa, there was a snowstorm. With that the two of them decided to skip the engagement process and get married on Monday. The rest, as they say, is history.

On Monday, Elias drove me to the D.C. airport and I caught my plane back to the opposite side of the country. Late that evening I landed in San Francisco. It was time for me to get back to my regular life as a college administrator, but after the whirlwind of my travels I felt like a new woman.

For the first time in my life since I was a child, I felt like anything was possible. As I reflected on the interviews I had done with Debbie Macomber who had published one hundred books while having dyslexia, Jon Regan who had sold five thousand albums as an independent musician, Kris Carr who was thriving with stage four cancer, and Eddie Fisher who had overcome homelessness to become the drummer for OneRepublic, I saw bits of myself in each of their stories. I realized the common denominator for all of my interviewees was that they pursued their dreams relentlessly against all odds. I couldn't help contemplate what would happen to me if I put my whole heart and soul into chasing a dream.

CHAPTER TEN
The Chase

On Tuesday morning I woke to the sounds of chirping birds and gobbling wild turkeys. There was something special about my on-campus apartment, nestled into the San Francisco suburb of Moraga, after all of the students had vacated for summer break. I had a particular morning routine. I turned on *The Today Show* right at seven, so that Ann Curry, Matt Lauer, and Meredith Vieira could fill me in on the latest news. While I listened, I made myself a pot of chai—half rice milk, half water, a few slices of ginger, a pinch of cinnamon, and a dash of masala.

I ran to my room to get ready until I heard a sizzling noise in the kitchen, alerting me that my chai had just boiled over and that it was piping hot and ready to be consumed. I would sit in my living room at the low Japanese-style table I had salvaged from a dumpster a few years earlier, devouring my breakfast and enjoying several cups of chai as I continued to watch *The Today Show*. I watched the camera pan over to Lenny, who stood on the sidelines just like always. It was strange to think that two days earlier I was standing beside him interviewing him. At 8:27 I finished my final cup of chai and began my two-minute walk to the office. During the summer I mapped out programs for the coming academic year about topics that ranged from healthy relationships to World AIDS Day awareness.

Just after four thirty, I got home in time to tune into the last half of *The Oprah Winfrey Show*. Oprah caught my attention just before she went to commercial break. She announced that she was looking for someone to launch his or her own show on her new network. The night before, I had gone to bed thinking about how to translate all of the recent content I had collected from interviews and experiences into a creative project or the pursuit of my own dream.

"Do you have what it takes?" Oprah asked. "Upload your video and tell me what your unique idea is and why you deserve your own show."

I immediately accepted Oprah's challenge as an invitation to revisit my childhood dream. I visited Oprah's "Your Own Show" website and quickly determined that I would compete in the wildcard category for a show I would call *Off the Beaten Path*. My show would feature people like those I'd encountered during the past year of my travels—people like Arga, the Balinese mother who took me to her village for the elections; Hummer, the Japanese artist who considered the world his oyster; Raj, the Punjabi expat worker who helped me find my way in Kuala Lumpur; Jon Regen, the jazz musician who made a name and a career for himself as an independent artist; and Lenny, the man who stood on the sidelines of *The Today Show* day after day for two decades.

I needed to produce a three-minute video to demonstrate the concept of my show, and I had to do it fast. My goal was to have my video finished and online for the world to vote on prior to the in-person auditions that were taking place in Southern California in ten days. Participants had the option of competing for their own show by posting a video or by going to an in-person tryout. I opted to do both.

First I had to scour through my video and audio files that were stored in my two laptop computers. Next I would need to write and refine a script, and finally I would need to piece it all together and post it online and accumulate as many votes as possible. That night I packed up my computers, my earphones, and my notepad and headed to Caffe La Scala in Walnut Creek to get started.

Anyone who is driven more by passion than practicality needs to have a safe haven just like Caffe La Scala. It's an Italian coffee shop with a full menu, mellow background music, and free Wi-Fi and attracts all sorts of creative types, students, and businesspeople. Over time I had developed an eclectic network of friends from the cafe who had started out as random people who struck up conversations with me while I worked on various projects. My geeky tech friend Aaron broke the ice with a conversation about the shop's delicious tomato soup. My friend Brandon had a practical day job but spent time in the café working on his side project of consulting single men on how to overcome dating obstacles and promoting gigs for the band he played in. James was a tall, bald, broad-shouldered massage therapist who spent time in the café designing a label for the massage oil line he was about to launch. These were the people I could talk to about my seemingly impractical pursuits, because they too were by all accounts impractical.

As I worked on this project, I did my best to blend into the background quietly drawing inspiration from the anonymous mix of coffee shop goers. I sat with my headphones on, staring at my computer screen, reviewing the audio and video footage of the past year of my life, while contemplating what to include in my three-minute video.

When I wasn't at Caffe La Scala, I sat at the table in the middle of my living room with my computers, audio files, and pads of paper scattered in front of me. I sometimes wondered what it would be like to be smugly satisfied with a less complicated life or to be one of those women who focused more on keeping a clean, organized home than pursuing pie-in-the-sky ventures. I avoided having any visitors in my apartment that week because I didn't want to explain the state of chaos or let anyone talk me out of my crazy idea.

I was finally making progress, getting ready to produce the on-camera portion of my video, and then Tuesday morning arrived. I had nothing against Tuesday, but on this particular Tuesday, I needed to fly to Las Vegas with three of my coworkers for a three-day conference. I was determined to have the bulk of my project finished prior to my departure from campus, but there was a perpetual difference in the amount of time any given task required in real time and the amount it required in my head. Minutes before my coworker pulled up to my apartment to pick me up, I realized I wouldn't meet my self-imposed deadline. Instead I quickly threw three dresses, two Macs, one PC, one camcorder, and one digital audio device into my suitcase. I was prepared to take my project on the road with me.

When I got to my hotel room in Las Vegas, I hung up my clothes and stuffed several pillows into the closet to create a little makeshift recording studio. I got up two hours before the sun rose each morning to work on writing, editing, producing, and reproducing my voiceover before attending the conference with my colleagues from eight a.m. onward. Every time I had a new version, I called my mom in Wisconsin, where she was on standby to offer me feedback on the updated editions of my project at all hours of the day.

After the conference ended on Thursday, I scurried to produce the on-camera portion of my video. The next day I would depart for Los Angeles to prepare for the in-person audition that would take place on Saturday morning in Laguna Niguel, California. My colleague brought a friend with her to the conference, and she had volunteered my room as a place for her friend to sleep during our last evening in Vegas. I asked my new inherited roommate to help me out, and she reluctantly agreed.

Finding a quiet place to do a video standup on the bustling, one-hundred-degree Vegas strip was not an easy task. Music blared out of seemingly invisible speakers. Sprinklers were running. There was constant traffic and large crowds of people. Finally we found a patch of grass surrounded by trees and a fence right in the middle of a hotel complex. We crawled in there and did no fewer than ten video takes, and two hours later we were finished. By now I had completed my script, done my voiceover, and shot the on-camera portion of my video audition. My final task was to weave it all together, carefully pairing up the audio with the right video and still-frame photos.

That evening my colleague and her friend were excited to have a girls' night out. I was walking a fine line. I was exhausted, sleep deprived, and in a mad rush to finish my video before the next morning, yet I felt obligated to join my friends. I left dinner a bit early so I could work on my video project, with the intention of joining them later. Once I got to my room, however, I knew I really needed to stay in and focus. When my two friends came to get me, I said I didn't think I could make it.

I knew from one of my friend's looks that my words were not well received.

"You promised," she said.

I felt guilty. Reluctantly, I threw on a dress to assuage my friends and went down to the overcrowded dance club that was connected to our hotel. I danced, drank water, and calculated how long I needed to stay with my friends to feel like I had participated wholly in the outing. I stayed for an hour and then hugged my friends goodbye. As I walked out of the club, exhausted and overwhelmed by the task that awaited me, I reminded myself that sometimes it's just not possible to please everyone and that sometimes you must take care of yourself first.

At two a.m. I walked back through the crowds of people in my little black dress and then cut through the casino— the only way to get back to my room. The casino was full of flashing lights. Some people were dressed head to toe in fancy designer clothing, while a handful of humbly dressed locals sat discreetly at machines, perhaps hoping to win big. For some this was an exciting place to be. For me it was depressing. No sunlight ever filtered through, so there was never any way of knowing if it was the middle of the night or the middle of the day. Each time my dad went through a manic episode with his mental illness, he ended up at a Wisconsin casino, where he lost track of time and lost count of the money he spent—money our family didn't have to spare. Life often felt out of control for my dad, so the casino perhaps represented a false source of hope or new possibilities in life. For this reason I always had hated casinos, so much that I didn't gamble a cent during my visit to Vegas.

I woke up at seven a.m. and forced myself to get out of my cozy bed. It was Friday, one day before the in-person auditions and seven hours before my flight to LA, and the pressure was on. I threw on some jeans, a top, and wedge shoes and headed down to the coffee shop to get to work. I pieced together video clips for three hours while I sipped coffee and picked at a crepe. After making some progress, I walked back through the center of overstimulation, the casino, to get to my room on the eleventh floor. I got into the same elevator as two good-looking men who appeared to be about the same age as me.

"Are you having a rough morning too?" one of them asked.

"No," I said, wondering if it was evident that I was sleep deprived and exhausted. Maybe I had bags under my eyes. I had only slept a total of eight hours in the past four days, so that would have been understandable.

"I'm actually doing really well today. How's your day going so far?" I asked with a friendly smile.

They looked at each other and shrugged. "It's all uphill from here," one of them said and smiled back.

I stepped out of the elevator and looked down at my shoes, and suddenly it all made sense. I had always loved shoes and considered them a good way to get a sense or at least a first impression of each person I encountered. I once went on a date with a man who had tassel loafers on. Tassel loafers aren't quite youthful enough for my tastes, and neither was the guy. Tennis shoes indicate an outdoorsy type. Loafers, in general, indicate a preppy type. Well-worn yet trendy shoes indicate someone who isn't afraid to put his or herself into the thick of life. The list goes on. I was most defined by my platform wedges; the platform offered a splash of edginess, but the wedge, in place of a pointed heal, gave me the kind of stability I needed to chase my pursuit of the moment. On that particular day, I had selected a pair of attractive wedges, or so I'd thought. The problem was that on my left foot, I had my black open-toed Paolo, which I'd picked up from a high-end consignment shop in Walnut Creek, and on my right foot I had a strappy gold wedge that had come from the American Cancer Society thrift store. I immediately took off my shoes and ran barefoot back to my room.

Yes, sleep deprivation officially had gotten the best of me. It was time for me to pack my bags, head to Los Angeles for the in-person audition, and get this crazy pursuit of a dream over with.

CHAPTER ELEVEN

Laguna Niguel via Manhattan Beach

That Friday afternoon I flew from Las Vegas to Los Angeles. I had made a pact with myself and set a deadline. I promised myself that I would have my video produced and uploaded to the Oprah Winfrey Network's "Your Own Show" website prior to the Saturday morning in-person audition in Laguna Niguel, California. Even though the in-person audition was optional, I wanted to show Oprah that I was serious about this. I had been meaning to visit my friends, Katrina and Geoff, the couple I had befriended in Ubud, Bali, a year earlier and who resided in Manhattan Beach, but never gotten around to it. The previous summer in Bali, Geoff and I frequently had exchanged tech equipment and advice so I could produce my stories in time for my radio deadlines, and I counted on Katrina for comic relief, not to mention photographing, videotaping, and offering her opinion on the project of the hour. Now that I was finally seeing them after a whole year, I was once again on deadline.

I picked up a rental car and headed to a Starbucks just down the street from Katrina and Geoff's Manhattan Beach home. While I waited for them to finish work, I checked out all sorts of hotel options. I hadn't yet figured out where I would rest my head that night.

As soon as I got the call from Katrina that she was done with work, I walked down to Manhattan Beach Avenue to meet her and Geoff in front of the Mexican restaurant where we would dine that evening. At six that June night, the sun still lit the sky as the ocean gently crashed along the shoreline, a warm breeze wafted my hair toward my face, and a mix of people lingered on the sidewalks. The place made me pause and breathe for a second longer.

Katrina and Geoff walked down the sidewalk, looking exactly as I had remembered them. Geoff was wearing flip-flops and swimming trunks, just as he always did, and Katrina wore a denim skirt, a yellow top, a pair of flip-flops, and an ear-to-ear smile. The couple offered to take me in for the weekend, and I humbly accepted the invitation. I felt like I needed a safe place to land.

I went to bed on the comfy couch in their beachside apartment by eleven that night. I was so tired that I felt lightheaded and off-center. Their beige-colored, cuddly, one-eyed cat, Jack, snuggled with me, and we slept like babies. In the morning I woke up early and started fresh. Katrina made a fantastic high-protein breakfast of eggs and soysage along with a potent cup of coffee, which I needed. I ate my breakfast and continued to work on the final details of my video.

The clock was ticking, the morning was slipping away, and I needed to make it to Laguna Niguel, a place that without traffic was an hour away. All participants had to be checked in before two p.m. to be considered for an in-person tryout. At twelve forty five p.m., I hit the "submit" button for my video and online application and then sprinted to my car.

On the drive I practiced telling Oprah's team why my show was worthy of being selected. I got to the Kohl's parking lot in Laguna Niguel in the nick of time, at one fifty p.m. To make this work, I needed to find parking, get myself to the check-in station, and get my wristband without a single glitch.

A woman in a blazing yellow jacket, who was directing traffic, stopped me. The way I would answer the question she was about to ask me would determine my fate for that day.

"Are you here for the Oprah Winfrey Network tryouts or to shop?" she asked.

"The tryouts," I replied.

"In that case, you're going to have to go around the block, turn right, and park in . . ." she went on to explain. My mind trailed off. I began to calculate the closest place I could park and make it to the tryout. By now it was 1:57 p.m.

Damn it, I said to myself. *I should have told her I was there to shop.*

I ended up parking in the Walmart lot just across the street from Kohl's. Ironically it was the exact parking lot the woman had attempted to direct me to before I panicked and tuned her out. By this point, though, it was 2:13 p.m. It wasn't looking good for me time-wise. I ran across the street and talked to the first security guard I met.

"Do you have a wristband?" she asked.

"No, not yet," I replied.

"Well, then, you can't come in. I'm sorry," she said.

"Is there anything I can do or anyone I can speak with?" I asked. Before she could respond, I stated my case. "You see, I flew in from Las Vegas late yesterday, spent the night in Manhattan Beach, rented a car, and drove all the way here. I'll leave my purse with you as collateral if you'll let me talk with someone," I pleaded.

"All right, keep your purse, but talk with those security guys up there, and they'll help you out." She pointed at the men in front of us.

I stated my case to the next two security guards. The two of them agreed to escort me to the tryout manager. I explained my situation to her too, but she was making no exceptions.

"I'm sorry," she said as she nodded her head. "There's nothing I can do." Even though I believe in persistence, I do consider three "no"s to equal a solid no.

Feeling completely deflated, I walked back through the blacktop Kohl's parking lot. My throat felt heavy as I attempted to hold back tears.

Damn it, I thought. *I should have come here first before finishing my video.*

I walked through the Walmart parking lot to my rental car with a heavy heart. I glanced up and couldn't believe my eyes. Dr. Ali Benizar, the author of *The Tao of Dating*, whom I had met and interviewed at the New York Book Expo two weeks earlier, was standing in front of me. I was glad to see a familiar face. The thought had crossed my mind that this was the type of thing that Ali would compete in, but I didn't follow up and ask him about it. I guess he had the same intuition about me. Ultimately we were friends, but we were also competitors. Before we parted ways, Ali invited me to join him at his white-dress birthday party, along with five hundred of his closest friends, which was taking place the next day.

I drove back to Manhattan Beach and picked up Katrina so we could go out for dinner and a drink and perhaps a small dose of shopping on the way. I needed to buy something white to wear to Ali's birthday party, and I definitely wanted a glass of wine.

Katrina and I walked down Manhattan Beach Boulevard toward the boutiques and restaurants. The sun was setting, surfers were working their way out of the water, and people trickled in and out of shops and bars. My interest was piqued by a boutique called All Yoo. The shop was owned and run by a Korean woman named Taem.

"Would you girls like some wine?" she asked.

Oh, you have no idea how much we'd like some, I thought. "Sure, I'll have a glass," I said politely, as if I were indifferent but open to the idea.

It turned out that Taem shared wine with many of her customers. She enjoyed drinking wine and thought it helped people relax, loosen up, and perhaps feel better about spending some money.

"I have an idea, Sharon," Katrina said. "Why don't you interview Taem?"

I almost always carried my audio recording device with me, but I didn't have it that particular night. I was fried, burned out.

"No worries, Sharon," Katrina said. "My iPhone has a built-in microphone."

With that, Taem shared her story of migrating from Korea to Los Angeles, marrying a white man, and finding a new level of freedom in owning her own business.

"I could never work for anyone else again. I like working for me," Taem said. She had a dream of creating her own line of clothing but was unsure what she should call her label.

After the interview, Katrina and I enjoyed some fantastic gluten-free pasta from a hole-in-the wall Italian shop and walked back to her home. In a way I felt relieved. I might not have had my tryout that day, but at least my video was uploaded. I'd made sure of that before I'd driven all the way to Orange County that morning. As soon as we got back to Katrina's home, I opened my computer so I could see how many votes I had received so far. I couldn't find my video, so I checked my e-mail. My heart sank when I opened the message from the network.

"Dear Sharon," it read. "Your video has been rejected because it displays logos or mentions brand names." Sure enough, I had mentioned the name of the radio station I worked for, the name of the college I worked at, and the name of a popular mainstream morning show. I also had accidentally shown a clip that included the Barnes & Noble logo in it. If only I had read the rules ahead of time, I would have known that logos and specific titles weren't allowed. I had one more glass of wine and decided to go to bed and start fresh the next day. I would need to reedit my video, reproduce my soundtrack, remix it, and upload it again. I had to do all of this before I could allow myself to catch my flight back to San Francisco, where my normal life awaited me.

When I woke up, it was Father's Day. As my mom, sister, brother-in-law, and niece grilled dinner for my dad in Wisconsin and my friends took their fathers out to brunch, I sat in Katrina and Geoff's Manhattan Beach apartment redoing the video I had already poured hundreds of hours of time and energy into. I wrapped up my project at 2:13 p.m., just as Katrina and Geoff returned home from their Father's Day outing. I didn't want to outstay my welcome, so I hugged and thanked both of them and headed out. Now all I had to do was find a high-speed Internet connection and upload the edited video. I ran down the street to Taem's boutique. I showed her the video, which now included some footage of her, and had her sign the handwritten release that authorized me to include a snippet of her interview in my final video. I was ready to rush off to the nearest coffee shop with Wi-Fi so I could upload my video and make a quick appearance at the white-dress party.

"Stay here, Sharon!" Taem demanded. "You work right here," she said as she pulled the Internet cord out of her computer and set me up behind her check-out counter. "I'll pour some wine for us."

I sat behind the counter in Taem's store, greeting customers who assumed I worked there. I was all set for the party, garbed in my white dress with gold trim and accessorized by a large black flower power ring I'd bought from Taem yesterday, but I doubted I would make it. Taem had no idea how pressured I felt to meet my self-imposed deadline, show up at the party, and make my flight home. She casually chatted, telling me more about her American husband who had fallen sick yesterday and contemplating the name for her line of clothing. Then she asked the inevitable question.

"Do you have a boyfriend?"

I told her that I dated a lot but hadn't found quite the right man. Taem looked confused, so I explained that men sometimes may have misconstrued my independent, free-spirited nature and that they perhaps saw me as the girl to hang out with while they were in transition or before they got into a "real" relationship. Just as I hadn't found one pair of shoes that matched all of my outfits, I hadn't found one man to go through life with. I had survived an abusive four-year relationship and ended an undefined three-year relationship, and I was only now learning to love myself. I was in no way desperate to settle for an "almost right" relationship again.

In the meantime I lived a pretty fantastic and free life. I had lots of strong, innovative friends, and I constantly came into contact with interesting people. While pondering this and chatting with Taem, I noticed that my video was taking forever to upload.

I texted Ali. "I don't know if I'll make it. I'm still finishing my video," I wrote.

He replied, "F-ck the video. You have a .001 percent chance of being selected for OWN, but there's a 100 percent guarantee you'll have fun here."

Just then I saw a lovely pop-up on my screen that read, "Your video has successfully uploaded." I shoved my two computers and my recording device into my bag, hugged Taem, and sprinted to my rental car in my little white dress and dependable wedges, and I was on my way to Sherman Oaks.

My GPS led me to a posh residential road with a mansion that overlooked all of Los Angeles. Cars were parked all the way up and down the winding road. Pedestrians sporting impeccable white attire walked to and from the party. I turned on my flashers and parked by the red curb that read NO PARKING ANYTIME, took a breath, and ran toward the house. By my calculations, I had exactly ten minutes to find Ali, wish him a happy birthday, take some pictures, greet a few people, and depart. That would leave me with just enough time to return my rental car and get to the airport thirty to forty minutes before my departure time. I rushed to the check-in table at Ali's gated party and explained that I wasn't on the list but indicated my chain of seven text messages from Ali insisting that I show up. I was in.

I fumbled through the crowd of hundreds of unfamiliar faces and found Ali dancing on a slab of cement near the pool.

"See. I made it! I have to leave right now, though, to make my flight," I said.

"You're not going to make it. Change your flight and stay a while," Ali cajoled.

"Can't," I said. I gave him a hug, a kiss on the cheek, wished him a happy birthday, and ran to my car. Unlike me, Ali worked for himself. He had shared that he was allergic to bosses when we had chatted during the New York Book Expo. I, however, depended on my job and my company-provided home, and I had to be back at work in precisely twelve hours.

Once I was in my car, it took a few minutes to get back out to the main road. There was a mix of drivers looking for parking; pedestrians walking up and down the road to or from the party of the man who happened to be the author of *The Tao of Dating*; and a few people like me who were trying to get the hell out of there. Just a hundred feet before the main road, there seemed to be a traffic jam for no apparent reason. I spotted a man with a white button-up shirt and dark hair waving his arms in the air. I opened my window.

"Look. I'm trying to leave. Let me out and then we won't be blocking traffic."

"I need your card," he said. "You're the most beautiful woman at the party, and I didn't get to talk to you." Of course, as it turned out, he hadn't even arrived at the party yet. Here's what he should have said: "You're one of the first women I saw here. I don't have much luck with women, so I'm going to meet as many of you as possible."

I rummaged through my purse, gave him my card, grabbed his, and hit the gas pedal. Every person I met was a source or a potential storyteller, and besides, I needed all the votes I could get for my Oprah audition video. I never looked at the man's card again and remembered nothing about him—not his face or his name.

During my mad dash to the airport, I called my sister and jokingly told her I might just have to head to Georgia the following weekend for the final in-person audition. The last Oprah Winfrey Network tryout was scheduled to take place in Roswell, Georgia, the very next Saturday. I closed my eyes at two thirty that Monday morning and went back to my normal life as a college administrator five hours later, but with a new level of passion and purpose.

CHAPTER TWELVE
Roswell, Georgia, or Bust

By the time I got back to work on Monday, my video was live for the world to see, and I needed to get as many votes as possible. It was hard to contain my excitement, but I went about my business—following up on e-mails, planning programs, and finishing my last month of work before July, my official unpaid month off. On Thursday afternoon I sat with colleagues from across the country, discussing ways to end gender-based violence, but my mind kept drifting off. The final in-person auditions for the Oprah Winfrey Network were taking place in thirty-six hours in Roswell, Georgia. Booking a last-minute flight to Georgia would cost as much as a flight to Japan. My stomach was filled with butterflies, the kind you feel when you're falling in love for the first time. Every fiber of my soul told me I had to go.

I called the travel agency in Minnesota I had used during my college years, and they were able to hook me up with a flight the next day for the bargain price of nine hundred dollars. By this point I didn't have enough money in my account to cover the flight. I humbly called my retired mother.

As I explained my predicament, I braced myself for any practical words of wisdom she might offer. I imagined something to the tune of "What the hell are you thinking?"

But she only said, "Well, then, you have to go, honey. I'll put it on my credit card, and you can pay me back later this summer."

Even though my mom and I bumped heads from time to time, as I think all mothers and daughters do, I admired her. As a former elementary school teacher and an active member of the small Wisconsin community of my roots, my mom was an inspiration.

When I turned seventeen and received a Kikkoman soy sauce scholarship to go to Japan, my mom held back her tears and gave me her blessing. When I was in college and wanted her to tell me what to do with my life, she repeatedly said, "You know what is best for you." Those words got under my skin, the way it does when someone scratches a chalkboard with their nails. Although I was frustrated at the time, I later realized she had instilled in me a strong core and the importance of looking within myself for answers.

When I began to travel the world as a non-tourist on a shoestring budget-—to volunteer, study, and pursue journalism projects in places such as Saudi Arabia's neighboring country of Qatar, the Tamil region of Sri Lanka, Cuba, Uganda, and India—my mom loved me enough to let me go. In January 2009, when I received a radio journalism fellowship and considered foregoing the opportunity because of my busy schedule even though it had been a dream of mine, my mom offered some wise words.

"Honey, I think it's worth making some time for this. I have a feeling this is something you'll love," she advised.

She was right. I quickly fell madly in love with radio reporting. As I worked on my Oprah pitch, my mom had been on call at all hours of the day and night to offer feedback. Now, when I was ready to hop on an overpriced flight to Georgia to see this dream all the way through, she gave me her blessing and lent me the funds to do it.

I knew many people who blamed their parents for their circumstances in life. Of course, as the product of our imperfect parents, we naturally inherit a bunch of issues. As I grew older, however, I realized I was infinitely blessed to have the parents I had. My mom, a teacher, married my dad, a janitor, at the age of thirty-five and brought me into the world just before she turned thirty-six. She was the first person in her family to go to college. My dad joined the Army when he was eighteen to get away from the farm where he had grown up. When he was offered the opportunity to complete a program to become a nurse, he opted out because he was worried about what other people would think of him. He instead spent his life working blue-collar jobs.

As I was growing up, my dad had a mental health issue that caused him to be hospitalized multiple times. Watching him navigate life in our small town, which was somewhat unforgiving of differences, had given me a heightened sense of empathy. It was my desire to understand what my purpose was and where I fit into the world that led me abroad and eventually to California. While home had felt like a chaotic place during my childhood, I was grateful for my experiences. If I were raised in a perfect family (which, by the way, I don't believe exists), I probably would have settled on a more comfortable life path and ended up living in my small town working as a banker or secretary. Although there's nothing wrong with those professions, I was convinced I had a different purpose. Fortunately, in my family, there was no pressure to keep up with the Joneses or marry by a particular age.

My flight was just twenty hours away. I still needed to finish my online application, stop by the consignment store to pick out an outfit for my in-person audition, and pack. I also was supposed to hang out in San Francisco that evening with Pete, a thirty-nine-year-old writer whom I had met at the New York Book Expo a month earlier. In retrospect it was a terrible idea to plan anything other than packing on that particular night. On my way to the city, a homeless spoken word artist and poet sat behind me and struck up a conversation before asking for money.

"I would," I started to say, "but today, I'm—"

"I don't need to hear your excuses," he snapped.

I was feisty that day.

"You didn't let me finish," I snapped back.

"Where are you from? I'm from Richmond. I bet you've never even been there."

Wrong. I went to Richmond all the time. It was right next to the San Pablo Contra Costa County Rape Crisis Center, the agency I partnered with for my day job and the place I had been earlier that day for training. It was where I had gone to cover the Richmond High gang rape case, which put Richmond on the map in 2009. I knew from my time there that a high rate of crime and hardship afflicted that city, but a great deal of creativity, compassion, art, invigoration, and community made up for some of the rougher parts.

By the end of the train ride, the spoken word artist and I connected. He told me that he was passionate about poetry, and that he gathered with a group of artists at the corner of 16th and Mission in San Francisco every Thursday night. He dropped his defenses and offered to do a spontaneous spoken word performance. He even worked our serendipitous encounter into an improv piece that he performed from his seat in the train while I recorded him on my audio device.

I've been known to rock this spot with some of the world's most talented and gifted.

I see that look in their eyes when I arrive at 16th and Mission.

I do what I do and I do it so swell.

If by chance something should happen and someone should go to jail,

we'll just pass this hat around and post the damn bail.

Some are shattered, torn, and emotionally twisted.

A whistle rings out loud and summons the crowd to attention.

Look! They have come, from far and near, to hear a few words from the tip of the tongue. No cause for alarm, all are multitalented and gifted.

If you step in this circle and stage, you best mind your own business.

If push comes to shove and shove comes to push, no cause for alarm, they just want a better look.

I rant and I rave in the circle and stage and look to the heavens above and I say, this has got to pay off soon someday.

I was blessed with a gift to reach down deep inside, grab and pull out what makes a crowd thrive.

Some stop, some stare, some sit and listen. Some walk by and smile, 'cause they're all so damn unique. They know what we're doing, and we're sure damn persistent.

Every Thursday night at nine, we arrive at 16th and Mission.

Some sing, some dance, and some just listen, but this is how we do it at 16th and Mission.

When he paused, I pointed my audio recorder back toward his face and asked him to introduce himself.

"Solo Artist," he said and then launched into another improv.

I'm the cat they dream about being. I'm going freestyle now. I'm on the BART, and I'm going platinum style. I'm with the girl with the blonde hair, and I'm ready to get down. What's your name? What you said? What was the platinum sound? While I'm kicking the sound?

What's your name?

Don't get stage fright right now.

What's your name, baby girl?

Do you hear what I'm saying?

Finally I got it. He needed me to tell him my name.

"Yeah, Sharon, right now, while I'm putting down the sound." Solo Artist continued with his rap until we reached Powell Station and I had to depart.

I bid my new friend goodbye and then grabbed a cab to meet Pete and his associates for dinner and a concert at a music venue called the Independent. To make a long story short, I missed the last train back to the East Bay and had to keep myself awake until five in the morning. At four forty five a.m., I stopped at Starbucks to grab some oatmeal for breakfast and caught the first train back. When I was on the train, in front of me I saw a middle-aged homeless man who had made himself a diaper out of plastic bags, which was wrapped around the exterior of his dirty blue pants, and a poncho out of another bag that he wore in place of a jacket. Even though I was starving minutes earlier, I suddenly lost my appetite. The man got off at the last San Francisco stop and another came in. This one was wearing a red winter jacket and carried a backpack. He sat in the seat beside mine and tried to have a conversation. He was deaf and mostly mute, so it was a challenge. I struggled to read his lips. His name was Lawrence, and he was on his way to Antioch. He was selling CDs for ten dollars. He gave me a paper that described a project that supported street musicians and artists. I offered him seven dollars for a CD called *Harmonic Humanity*, because that's all the cash I had and I was genuinely intrigued. He smiled and drifted off to sleep. When I reached the Walnut Creek Station where I had left my car, I squeezed his arm, smiled, and waved goodbye.

I drove home to Moraga then quickly packed and got ready for work. I threw some essentials into a suitcase, and this time I brought only one mini-computer that fit into my purse, my audio device, a few changes of clothes, and the *Harmonic Humanity* CD I had purchased on the train. I threw my bag into my car and headed to the office. I was running on empty, as I hadn't even slept a minute the night before. After work I rushed to the airport and once again got there just in time to board my plane.

By the time I picked up my car from the Atlanta airport, drove to Roswell, and checked into my hotel, it was one a.m.

Six hours later, at seven a.m., I was being corralled into line in yet another Kohl's parking lot, along with thousands of other excited contestants. I stood behind a magician who had driven all the way from Mississippi and in front of a woman who had driven from North Carolina. I received a magical plastic purple bracelet that served as my ticket to get access to the tryouts and was assigned a five p.m. audition time. I went back to my hotel to pass another eight hours.

At the hotel I went straight to the hot buffet breakfast. A group of forty- and fifty-somethings invited me to join their table. I could tell by the purple bracelets on their wrists that they were here for the same purpose I was. Among them was a man from New York City who was a real estate agent by day and a motivational speaker on the side, as well as a colorful, vibrant, and flamboyant woman from Florida who hosted a radio show called *Best Life Barb*. The group took turns sharing what it meant to be auditioning for the Oprah Winfrey Network and talked about the risks they had taken to get here and what they hoped to get from the experience. I felt a little like I was sitting at a "follow your dreams" support group, but I was inspired by how committed they all were.

After about thirty minutes, I excused myself so I could rest and further prepare for my try-out. I needed to print out my online application and bring it with me to the in-person audition, which meant I had to start from scratch. I told the receptionist about my predicament, and she allowed me to go behind the check-in counter and print the eighteen-page application. I went back to my room, took a nap, touched up the curls in my hair, refined my script, and practiced in the mirror repeatedly.

I grew up in a working class family in a small town in Wisconsin. When I turned seventeen, I craved for a world that was larger than the one that I knew, so I applied for a Kikkoman soy sauce scholarship, which transplanted me out of Wisconsin and into the heart of Tokyo. I've been traveling and interviewing people ever since. Because I know everyone has a story to share, a lesson to teach and a dream, I never go anywhere without my recording device, I said. Then I went on to mention three of my most recent serendipitous encounters that had turned into intriguing interviews.

In my show I'll take you off the beaten path and introduce you to people whose stories you haven't heard before, people who are pursuing passion over practicality and people who have used failure as a springboard to reach the next goal in life. This show will inspire you to find your rhythm and to embrace change.

When I left my room, I felt confident and ready to tell the world why my show should be chosen for the Oprah Winfrey Network.

As I walked out the door of the hotel, the receptionist wished me good luck. "Keep it under thirty seconds, don't talk about yourself, and you'll do great," she said. "Another participant told me that's the trick."

I felt like a rug had just been pulled out from under me. I had been working all day on keeping my pitch to one minute, and my pitch definitely included me. I ran into two other participants—one who said, "Keep your pitch to two sentences" and another who said, "Be careful so you don't get cut off." I stood in my callback line with the eleven other people in my group and considered the best way to cut myself out of my pitch.

The casting director came and met my line and directed us to the far-right tent, where we were instructed to give a pitch no longer than thirty to forty-five seconds and to avoid sharing our life stories. "Those of you who make the cut will get your callback this evening," he advised. "Good luck."

I watched the twelve participants in my group, one-by-one, stand up and make their pitches. I may have appeared to be listening to them, but really I was actively contemplating what I would say when it was my turn.

"Next," the casting director said.

I stood up, still not knowing what I would say. *This is it*, I told myself. I took a deep breath and started. "My name is Sharon Sobotta. I grew up in the small, working-class town of Whitehall, Wisconsin. When I was seventeen, I was rescued by a Kikkoman soy sauce scholarship."

I kept talking after this, but I was so anxious and sleep deprived that I don't recall what I said. And then I completely blanked out and froze.

The casting director looked up. "That's it?" he asked.

After a brief mental sabbatical, I reentered consciousness.

"Umm, no," I said. I turned and reached into my handbag and pulled out my audio recorder so I could use it as a prop, and I continued. Even as I was speaking, I was still trying to calculate the best way to take myself out of my story.

"Because I know everyone has a story and I never know who I'm going to run into, I never go anywhere without my recording device. This is a show about people who have used failure as a springboard for reaching the next goal, tragedy as opportunity, and about people like you—people who are doing their part to make the world a better place."

I made it through the audition, but I knew in my heart that I didn't shine the way I could have.

Right after I finished, the two women sitting beside me shared their idea for a deaf soap opera in sign language, as an interpreter verbalized their ideas. Both of the women talked about the need for deaf people to be seen, honored, and valued in society. One talked about doing a show focusing on what people can do—not on what they can't do—while the other proposed a reality show of sorts, so that people could see deaf people in mainstream America. In that moment I had a flashback of my encounter with the deaf man who had sold me a CD a day earlier. I brought that CD with me to Georgia and played it in my rental car as I traveled from place to place. It occurred to me that in my lifelong quest to give voice to people from all walks of life, I had missed out on an entire group of people. I never had given voice to a deaf person—not literally, not figuratively. I needed to change that immediately.

As soon as my audition group was finished, I turned to the interpreter for the two deaf women and requested an interview. I asked the questions and the interpreter signed them. They responded in sign language, and she verbalized their answers for me.

"My name is Deanna," the first woman told me. "I am twenty-six years old. I came here to the Oprah audition to pitch a show called *Living Through the Eyes of Silence*, a deaf soap opera. I want to give the world an opportunity to come and join our world and experience what life is like when you're living without sound, when you're working with people who deal with sound, and learning how people who live without sound live, how they work, how they have relationships."

"What's the most challenging aspect of being deaf in this society?" I asked.

"For me the hardest part is that they don't treat you the same as they treat other people. They treat deaf people like we're from a different world. We want to experience life and become a part of America's mainstream if the hearing world will open up and let us."

"What's your dream?" I asked.

"I want to be a fashion model," she replied.

Deanna was slim, tall, and easily could have been a fashion model.

"What's the most important lesson you've learned in your life?" I asked.

"I established in my mind that if I see something, I can do it. There is nothing that is impossible for me because I'm deaf. It's not an excuse. I can accept that I can go out and do anything and give it my best."

Next it was Evaan Black's turn. She was a heavy-set, resilient woman wearing a suit. She introduced herself and shared that she was forty-eight years old and from Alabama. By this point the interpreter was tired and anxious to get going, so I kept the interview short.

"What's the most important lesson you've learned on your life journey?" I asked.

"I've learned to accept who I am and to not let people tell me who I am or what my life should be," she said. "I don't let people tell me I'm disabled. I am able. I can do anything but hear. I can cook. I can drive. I have a college degree, two PhDs. You can't tell me that I can't do anything. I've learned to be myself as a black deaf woman, and I can do anything I want to do. That is what my mom taught me, to love myself for who I am," she signed with conviction.

I asked her about her job. The interpreter struggled to decipher her long title, but Evaan kept trying until she had communicated it successfully. "I am the State Coordinator of Deaf Technology Services with the Alabama Department of Rehabilitation Services."

As I drove back to the hotel after my interview with the two women, I realized I had totally misunderstood the producer's instructions to avoid sharing our life story as a command to take ourselves out of our pitches. I couldn't take "me" out of my story because I was my story.

In that moment I knew I had come a long way. I had become a journalist years earlier so that I could always deflect attention from myself, because at that time I saw my own narrative as irrelevant. Now my prop for getting people to open up and share their stories with me was me. I was suddenly proud of my humble beginnings, because I understood that they set my context. I no longer saw the details of my own life as irrelevant. I finally had learned to love myself.

CHAPTER THIRTEEN
The Waiting Game

On my way back to the hotel, I got a call from Heidi, the mother from North Carolina who had been corralled into the same line as me that morning. She invited me to join a few of the OWN competitors who were having appetizers and drinks at a restaurant called Brookwood Grill. I knew the chance of my getting a callback was slim, but I figured I might as well wait it out in the company of others who were in the same boat. As I chatted with my competition in the dimly lit, bustling bar and eatery, I couldn't help notice the two hipster-looking house musicians—one with wavy blond hair and a vest and another with spiky brown hair and glasses and a flannel shirt—setting the tone with mellow acoustic cover songs. I guess they must have noticed me attentively watching them as I listened to their music, because as soon as they took a break, they came over and introduced themselves. They were Austin Adams and Nick Pirtle. Of course I interviewed them.

Austin shared that he had fallen in love with music as a kid and thought it might be something he would enjoy pursing for the rest of his life. At the time he was working on a six-song album that was influenced by groups such as Cold Play and British musicians.

"This whole project is about showing people that among the muck, the dirty, and everything we have to deal with, life never comes at a pace we can't handle. Call it God, fate, or chance—there is always some force out there that tells us things will eventually work out for the better," Austin explained.

Hours later, when I returned to the hotel and stopped at the Internet station in the middle of the lobby, there was one participant who was critiquing the producer who had judged her group. Another participant was debating whether she should put her pitch online. When she spotted me, she actually got on the phone and called her mom to tell her she was sitting beside the woman who had pitched the show titled *Off the Beaten Path*. That humbled me. The woman then turned and talked to me about her dilemma. She was afraid that if she posted her idea, someone else might steal it.

"Um, I'm pretty sure Oprah doesn't need to take your idea," I said.

"Yeah, but what would you do if you had an idea and you thought it was really good? Would you put it out there for the world to see or would you keep it?" she asked.

"I *did* have a unique idea. I think it's really good and I *did* put it out there for the world to see. I think it's a risk worth taking."

I settled into my room that evening and watched my clock turn to ten thirty, then eleven, then eleven thirty, and then twelve. I clearly wouldn't be getting a callback for a second in-person audition. However, I still had an online video in the running, and I had learned a lot from the experience. Finally, at one a.m., my phone rang, and it was a Georgia number. "Thank God!" I said out loud. It turned out not to be the producer but instead Emily Smith, an author from Georgia whom I had interviewed at the New York Book Expo a month earlier after I had spotted the catchy cover of her book, *Thank You Mr. Wrong.* She had received my Facebook message that I was in town and was calling to coordinate a time to meet.

The next morning I ran into Heidi again. She got teary-eyed as she shared that she too did not get a callback. As the mother of two, Heidi revealed that she thought she needed to take the creative risk, not only for her own sake but also for the sake of her children. Heidi was an oil painter who found inspiration for her artwork in various sources of light. She got her idea for the Oprah Winfrey Network a week earlier, when she was lying on her mat in a yoga class as the instructor read a passage from Oriah Mountain Dreamer's book, *The Invitation.* Heidi gave me her pitch that morning in the hotel lobby.

"Have you ever thought about the one thing we all have in common, the one thing we all long for? It is quite simply purpose. Many of us are pounding the pavement trying to get a job or working at jobs we're ridiculously over qualified for. We are less and less satisfied with our lives. I'm pondering how this concept would translate to a show and then I go to a yoga class. My teacher recited this passage from *The Invitation*:

It doesn't interest me what you do for a living. I want to know what you ache for. I want to know if you are willing to dream of meeting your heart's longing. It doesn't interest me how old you are. I want to know if you are willing to look like a fool for the sake of love, your dream, or the adventure of being alive. (Oriah, 2006)

"As I laid there in a sea of goose bumps, I had what Oprah would call an 'a ha' moment. And I knew I wanted to do a show about exactly that—a show to help people find their purpose," Heidi explained with moist eyes.

I asked Heidi what she had gained from the whole experience.

"I think it's a beautiful thing for your children to see you putting yourself out there. It teaches them that it is okay to take risks."

She explained that painting and helping others paint was her purpose.

"And then there's people like you . . . running around trying to chase your dream—of sharing other people's stories, trying to give voice to others by interviewing them—that you are already living," she said with a smile.

I didn't put much thought into Heidi's final comment. Instead I hurried to my room to gather my things and prepare for my final day in Georgia. I stopped at the Internet station one last time before beginning my drive to Atlanta.

There was a woman in her fifties with short gray hair and a striped shirt emblazoned with the words "Brooklyn, New York." She spoke with me about her audition. Her name was Esmaralda and she had come to Georgia to pitch a show called *Get Your Wellness On*. She got her idea for the show while dealing with the pain of losing her son, who was a student at NYU when he jumped to his death off the tenth floor of the library.

"Suicide messed with the wrong mother. I went after it. Advocacy, speaking, and writing helped me get back up on my feet. And in the course of doing that, I've come across a lot of other people who also have a story to tell. Being heard, I've come to believe, can be part of the healing process. This is how the idea for the show came to me," she explained.

Esmaralda's son Andrew was a twenty-year-old junior who was majoring in East Asian studies and studying Chinese at the time he died. She described him as a gorgeous human being, both inside and out, as she listed some of his most endearing qualities.

"My son, Andrew, found culture fascinating He was an observer. He was an incredible judge of character. He spoke when he needed to, and he listened more than he spoke. When he did speak, he said illuminating things. He was an incredible mimic and had an extraordinary sense of humor. He was very intelligent. I adored him. He drove me nuts as well."

"What's the most important lesson you learned from losing your son to suicide and going through your own healing journey?" I asked.

"There is no end to the kind of pain you can feel," Esmaralda said. "Yet there is no end to your strength and to the life that you can still live. You can still feel the pain, and you can die of it, or you can feel the pain and acknowledge it and move it. We are incredibly powerful individuals. I hope that everyone can learn that and carry on living. I choose to see the positive if I can. I know that as much as the pain has ripped me apart—and still rips me apart—at the same time, it's given me such a depth. I know that I can feel. I'm certainly not shallow. Would I have wanted to learn this in a gentler, more joyful way? Yes, I would have preferred that. But I also know that I am grateful to have had my son. I would go through it again just to feel that love. My love is even stronger now than it was before."

As I parted ways with Esmaralda, I felt like the universe was working some incredible magic that day.

CHAPTER FOURTEEN

Hot-Lanta

My final day in Georgia was ticking away, and I wanted to make my last hours count. I decided to let my GPS determine my fate for the day. As soon as I got into my car, I typed "vegetarian restaurant" into the GPS and randomly selected an eatery called Soul Vegetarian.

I arrived at a place that felt very similar to my old neighborhood in East Oakland, California. I parked in an empty lot beside the restaurant I was looking for, in front of a CVS store and directly across from a Goodwill. I got out of my car and walked to the restaurant, where someone met me at the door and pointed at the sign. "We are closed," he mouthed.

A tall man in a maroon-and-yellow suit and a matching hat walked across the street to talk to me. I asked him for a recommendation. He offered to walk me to a purportedly amazing vegan restaurant called Healthful Essence. The man's name was Yoseka. He called himself a Hebrew Israelite, not to be mistaken for a man of any particular religion, as he was quick to note, because he saw religion as something that divided people. He told me that he had learned from a failed relationship to be more patient and less aggressive. As we stood in the piping-hot sun, sweat dripped off Yoseka's face, but he shared a piece of his own narrative.

"I am part of a community of African Hebrew Israelites from Jerusalem," he said. "When we first left America in 1967, we stayed in West Africa and Liberia in the jungle, and we lived there for two-and-a-half years in tents, cleansing ourselves of all of the negativity that we experienced throughout the four hundred years living in America. We are here in Atlanta working to support our nation and community that's in Israel. We, who are the Hebrews, are not Jewish. We don't practice any religion."

On a more personal note, Yoseka shared that he had learned his most valuable life lesson when his wife had left him.

"I learned that I have to be more patient when dealing with sisters [women]. I have to be less aggressive. All of my life I've been a hard brother and when I met this sister [his ex-wife], I didn't know any other way to be. That turned into something else—physical and verbal aggression. I'm trying to make some changes. I've learned that a lot of times when things are happening, you shouldn't say anything. You should leave it be and see the type of response you get from just not saying anything. A lot of times you can talk too much, and that will mess up things. Now I'm happy to be alive and healthy."

After the interview I shook Yoseka's hand and headed into Healthful Essence. There was a full menu of items:

"ungoat" curry, curried tofu, roti, and other items I might find at a stall in Bangladesh or India. I settled on quinoa, vegetarian curry, a side of curried tofu, and a fresh cup of tea. I was intrigued. I was in an inner city neighborhood, but vegetarianism had caught on here to the point that it was sort of uncool to eat meat. The owner, a tall, thin woman named Princess Dixon, had taken up veganism two decades earlier after reading that meat causes people to get old prematurely. She had found her life's purpose in the art of cooking. I asked what the most rewarding and interesting parts of running a vegan restaurant in the heart of Atlanta were.

"The most interesting thing is that when people leave, their plates are very clean! I feel good when people tell me that they enjoyed their food. I love to cook. Food is my passion," she explained with a wide smile.

Just as Princess Dixon had said, by the time I left, my plate was clean and my belly was full.

On the way to my car, I swung into Goodwill for a quick round of shopping. Thirty minutes later I left with two pairs of shoes, a new denim skirt, a red-and-pink plaid top, and a pair of jeans. There was one small problem. I had to figure out a strategic way to fit my new items into my tiny suitcase. I opened my trunk and got inside so I could make room for my ever-expanding wardrobe. I closed the suitcase and then sat on it as I tried to force the zipper to close. I was totally involved in what I was doing—so focused that I was completely startled when a man started to speak to me. I looked up and saw it was a watermelon salesman who had converted his pickup truck into a melon produce market just across the parking lot.

"How you doin'?" he asked. "My name is Max. Just wanted to see if you needed any melons."

It was a comical question, but I imagine I must have looked like quite a spectacle as I sat in my trunk that hot afternoon. I had a little bit of time before my flight, so I thought I should find out more about the melon man.

"Hi, Max. Nice to meet you," I said. "I'll be right over to check out your melons, and if you're up for a quick interview, that would be great."

Max had been a real estate guy before the economy crashed, and now he was sustaining himself by selling produce. People heading to CVS randomly stopped by to look at the melons, and Max made sure to get the attention of those who appeared not to notice him.

"Three dollars for the little ones, five for the big ones. Feel free to take a look. I'll pick out a good one for you," he told the customers.

As I was getting ready to walk back toward my car after talking to Max, a man walked up to the pickup truck. I thought he was coming to buy fruit, but as it turned out, he was coming to talk to me. He could tell by my audio recorder that I was a journalist. There had been a homicide just down the road, and there was going to be a candlelight vigil that evening. Since I was a reporter, he invited me to cover it. Although I had to decline because I had a flight to catch, I convinced the man to let me interview him. The man's name was Pastor Kenneth Glasgow, and he was Al Sharpton's brother.

Pastor Kenneth Glasgow was the national president of TOPS, The Ordinary People Society. He was on his way back from the United States Social Forum in Detroit and had a van full of young people waiting for him as we talked.

Kenneth explained that he and his organization were preparing for a vigil for Terry Moody, an eighteen-year-old local artist who was shot dead the previous night while performing at a block party.

"He just graduated from high school. He was a beautiful young man. We are going to say 'Enough is enough.' We are tired of all the senseless and useless killings of each other," Kenneth said.

"How big of a problem do you think inner city youth violence is?" I queried.

"It's bad enough that so many young black men are going to jails and prisons by statistics and per capita, but then we also have to deal with the problem of them killing each other as well. Youth violence seems to be on the rise in this community," he explained.

Kenneth revealed that he had spent more than fourteen years in prison for drug and burglary charges. He wasn't able to be present for his son the way that he thought a father should be. He admitted that he changed his name from Kenneth Sharpton to Kenneth Glasgow because he didn't want to bring shame to his family or to his brother. When Kenneth got out of jail and wanted to get his life back on track, he found that it was even harder than he had imagined.

"I got out and I wanted to get a job, a house, and wanted to get an education, and I couldn't because I was disenfranchised," he explained. "When a person loses their voting rights—as they do in many states after they are classified as a felon—it's not just about voting. You can't get a loan; you can't get financial aid for college; you can't get a business license; you can't get public housing, public assistance, or food stamps if you've got a drug charge. God gave me a second chance, and society should do the same. Labeling people as felons causes collateral consequences in order to survive. I don't understand why we would make policies and laws to keep a person disenfranchised. It would cost only one-third as much as the prison systems to get someone treatment who has drug addiction. And then you're committing harm reduction."

Kenneth's organization was in the midst of a "remove the box" campaign, so that felons could regain the right to vote and access other basic rights so they could have a voice in society. He went on to tell more about the philosophy of his organization, The Ordinary People Society.

"The reason we feed people in my organization is because I know from experience—if you feed me, it dissipates my high, I come down, I won't rob you and I won't go in your house. If you help me get an education, then I'll become a productive citizen. It says in the bible, every seed produces of its own kind. If you're a productive citizen, produce some productive citizens."

I asked him what the rhythm of change meant to him and how it applied to his life. At the time I was still working on my blog called "The Rhythm of Change," and Kenneth seemed like an ideal candidate to offer some insight.

"Ooooh. C'mon now! I like that!" Kenneth gushed. "In order for us to be an arch bender, for us to be a life changer, for us to be in the beat of the rhythm of change, we have to realize that we're not soldiers. Soldiers can go AWOL. They can sell out. We have to become warriors. A warrior goes by instinct. It's instilled in him/her, not only to be comfortable in fighting the war zone but to protect everyone else around him/her."

Kenneth Glasgow and his youth team headed off to the candlelight vigil to pay tribute to Atlanta's latest homicide victim, and I walked across the parking lot to bid Max farewell. By now my jeans were sticking to me in the humid air, and my mouth was parched from the combination of the heat and the nonstop interviewing I'd done for the past few hours. Max told me a melon would help hydrate me. I decided it would be too inconvenient for me to try to get a melon on the plane with me, but I wanted to keep my word. "This isn't going to fit in my luggage, but I want to buy this for him." I pointed at the homeless guy who was leaning up against the CVS.

"No. I don't need charity," Max told me. "If you don't need one, it's totally cool."

"Seriously, Max. This isn't about you. It's totally about me, and I need some good karma."

"Fine. I'll let him pick one out," Max said with a smile.

As I drove away, I realized that my purpose in flying all the way to Georgia had been defined much more by the serendipitous encounters I'd had that weekend than by the Oprah Winfrey Network tryout. It didn't matter what happened with my pitch for *Off the Beaten Path* for Oprah's new channel. Being off the beaten path was simply my way of life. Don't get me wrong—having a spot on the Oprah Network would have been a pretty awesome way to give voice to a diverse range of people and share their stories with the world. But I had to marvel at the experiences I had collected in this short span of time. While chasing my dream, I had found an artist on a mission to help others live with purpose, a woman who used the devastation of losing her son as inspiration to help others get well, two deaf women who reminded me that even people who can't speak need to be heard, a vegan chef who tried to help her community get healthy, and a range of other colorful personalities. Because I had taken the time to interview Max, the melon man, I had the chance to meet Al Sharpton's brother. The experience reminded me that no story is too small to be told and reiterated the fact that the universe does have a plan for us if we allow it to unfold.

CHAPTER FIFTEEN
Fourth of July Weekend

Fourth of July weekend came, and I finally felt I could let my hair down and relax. I had done all I could do for the Oprah Winfrey Network competition. My fate was totally in the hands of voters. If enough friends, acquaintances, and strangers visited the site and cast their vote for *Off the Beaten Path*, I still had a chance.

After taking a long sabbatical from my weekend reporting gig at KPFA, I had agreed to a full weekend of work for the station. I spent Saturday at an Oakland-based conference about socialism, where I interviewed a few Puerto Rican student activists about their quest to make education accessible to the masses. Not so ironically, I had committed my Sunday to producing a piece called *Off the Beaten Path*, which featured several of the powerful and inspirational women I had interviewed the previous weekend in Georgia for *Women's Magazine*, KPFA's weekly Monday show.

On Sunday my co-producer from *Women's Magazine* at KPFA graciously allowed me to work from home. My vision was that I could do a little bit of script writing, audio editing, voiceover production, and a lot of cleaning in my apartment. I had neglected my living space for the past month. The table in the center of my living room was filled with papers, notes, and audio memory cards. My suitcase was in my bedroom waiting to be unpacked. My closet was exploding. My laundry had piled up. My home felt like a war zone. I started to clean in the morning but found plenty of ways to distract myself. Every ten minutes I checked Oprah's page to see how many votes my video had accumulated. When I finally found a good rhythm, I heard the little pop sound that accompanied a new Facebook chat message. It was Nick, my Facebook friend from Greece. Though we had never met in person, we routinely had deep philosophical conversations about life, happiness, and yoga.

"You're creating your own reality," Nick told me. "If you want a clean house, you'll have one. Imagine having a clean space and it will happen."

"Okay, Nick. I'm imagining it and it's not happening," I typed jokingly.

I knew what he meant, though. If having an organized living space was something I valued, I had to move that up the hierarchy of priorities and make it happen.

When my sister and I were children, we designed clever games for cleaning the house. We imagined our house to be a store. One of us would shop for a hundred items and then we'd go through the checkout line before putting everything away. After putting the items away, we always took a break for a snack. I decided to try out that time-honored technique just for the hell of it. I got to number twenty-five before my phone rang. When I answered I heard a nasally voice on the other end. It was the crazy man who had flagged me down after Ali's party in Los Angeles two weeks earlier. I was shocked that he had called me.

"Hi, Sharon. This is Barry. I'm an attorney. I met you at a party, and I need to take you to dinner." He seemed unfazed when I told him I lived in San Francisco. "Well, you're going to have to let me fly you to LA, because we need to have dinner together. Maybe I can fly you over later today, and we can party together for the Fourth of July," Barry insisted.

I declined, but he was persistent.

We finally reached a compromise. I was scheduled to go back to Manhattan Beach before flying to Wisconsin to spend time with my family in a few days. I suggested we meet for dinner when I was in Southern California. When he asked about my taste in food, I let him know I could go anywhere that had vegetarian and gluten-free options. He immediately offered two dinner choices. The first was a trendy restaurant in West Hollywood that was famous for prime rib. The second, Mangiamo, an Italian restaurant that served lots of floury, gluten-filled pastas, was a few blocks from where I would be staying in Manhattan Beach. Clearly he wasn't listening when I shared that I didn't eat meat or wheat.

Before I could even think about my date with this strange man, I needed to begin to produce my stories. Cleaning would have to wait. I cleared off some space on my living room table and edited my interviews to five minutes each. Then I went into my closet to produce my voiceover. By the time I finished all of that and sent my story to my co-producer, it was already four p.m.

Instead of getting back to cleaning, I poured myself a glass of red wine, sat on my cushy couch, put my feet up on my cluttered table, took a breath, and relaxed. Although the weekend was technically almost over, it felt like it was just beginning for me. My month off of work was about to begin. Other people would head back to work tomorrow, but I would sleep in, have coffee at Caffe La Scala, and then take my time packing my bags for my trip to Wisconsin via Manhattan Beach. A couple of hours later, after a much needed nap, I went online to check my vote count. I had received a few dozen more votes since I had last checked, and I also had attracted a hater with poor grammar.

YOU WANT FAME AND MONEY USING POOR PEOPLE AND SUFFERING CHILDREN WHO NEED FOOD AND WATER TO SURVIVE!!!!!!!!!! INSTEAD OF TRYING TO BE FAMOUS YOU MUST SEE THE FEELINGS OF A HUNGRY CHILD SMILING WITH A PIECE OF BREAD, A HAPPY TEAR OF A MAN SEEING HIS WIFE AFTER A HARD DAY OF WORK AND HAVE A BOWL OF RICE FOR A MEAL!!!!!!!! GROW UP AND IF YOU REALLY CARE ABOUT THESE PEOPLE, SHOW THEM THAT YOU CARE BY LEAVING THEM ALONE OR GIVE THEM FOOD AND TEACH THEM HOW TO READ!!!!!!

After years of practice receiving critical feedback as a writer, a reporter, and a college administrator who worked with marginalized populations, I considered myself an expert in not taking things personally. As a woman who had just chased a dream from Las Vegas to Los Angeles to Georgia, I would have expected myself to let this disparaging comment roll right off my back, but really I was devastated. I called my friend James for a pep talk.

James was one of the people who had befriended me at Caffe La Scala months earlier, when he happened to sit beside me while he was designing a logo for his massage oil line. He assured me that the random comment from the stranger was clearly written by someone who missed the point, and he encouraged me to let it go.

After I got off the phone with James, I crafted a response to my detractor.

I resisted every temptation to correct the commenter's assumptions line by line. I don't come from money, nor did I have a lot of it, nor was I interested in it or driven by it. I had taught refugee children in Sri Lanka and cared for dying patients in India. I bought meals for homeless people in my own community every chance I got. I wanted to lambast the commenter about his sexist remark about the happy tear of the man who saw his wife after a full day of work. What about the man's wife, who was probably working all day at home? What about me, for God's sake? Instead I just wrote this.

I'm sorry that you misunderstood the premise of my idea and pitch. I have been doing this work for more than a decade, and it is not about fame or money. I disagree with you that the best way to help poor people is to "leave them alone." I do think that everyone—regardless of their socioeconomic status or national, ethnic, or racial identity—has a story that needs to be heard.

At about ten p.m., I heard a series of rumbles in the sky. I peeked through my blinds to catch a glimpse of fireworks, only to discover that the trees surrounding my building blocked my view. I shut my blinds, wrapped myself in a cozy blanket, and called it a night.

CHAPTER SIXTEEN
An Odd Detour

On Wednesday afternoon I was back in Manhattan Beach, sifting through my dress options with Katrina in preparation for dinner with Barry. I was going to dinner with him only because I had agreed to do so, and now I just wanted to get it over with.

"Nope, he'll like that one too much," we said about the purple V-neck option.

"No, I can't wear this one. I was wearing a white dress the day he chased after me to get my number," I said about my white dress, fresh from the local thrift store.

"Perfect!" we said in unison, when I modeled my green, knee-length flowing dress with cap sleeves and no sign of cleavage.

I had a knot in my stomach, not a knot of excitement or anticipation but a knot of dread, when I left Katrina's beachfront apartment that evening. I walked slowly, watching the waves pound into the sand of Manhattan Beach in the setting sun just a block to my left. I called my friend Alex in Long Island for a quick pep talk.

"Alex," I said, "I'm going to dinner with a criminal defense attorney who speaks like Borat and who I should have said no to. Check on me later tonight."

Alex and I frequently provided moral support to each other as we navigated the dating world. Alex had gone through all the men in my life along with me—Joe, the divorcee in a dead-end factory job in Wisconsin; the short one we nicknamed "Mr. Clean" with a shiny bald head and glasses; Sam, the cheap one, who spoke in baby talk and gave me a teddy bear with a candy cane and a Santa hat attached to it for Valentine's Day; Ed, the European musician who frequently let me know he was wiser than me because of our age difference; Blake, the restaurant owner who wore loafers; Ravi, the guy I loved in college who waited until he was married to someone else to let me know that he loved me too; and most recently Pete, a photogenic, talented writer from the East Coast who was perfect in all ways except that maybe our pheromones didn't match—because even showers didn't make his body odor go away.

I finished leaving Alex a message just in time to stop by and see Taem at All Yoo, the clothing boutique I had visited to find the dress I'd worn to Ali's birthday party, which was also where I had met the man I was about to dine with.

Taem remembered me and gave me a big hug.

"I watched the video every day and voted for you, Sharon," she said effusively.

"Taem, I'm going to dinner with a guy, and I think I shouldn't. But I came early so I could say hello to you," I said.

"No, you should go. It's good," Taem insisted. She reached for my dress. "Here. Let me unbutton one. It's sexy that way."

I explained that there was no need to be sexy, that this was not a man to look sexy for. My plan for the evening was to keep dinner short and sweet and then get back to Katrina's home as early as possible.

Just before eight p.m., I arrived at Mangiamo, a quaint Italian restaurant a half-block from the beautiful moonlit ocean. Barry hadn't made reservations (as he told me he had), but there were plenty of tables available, so I went ahead and secured one. The hostess led me to the very rear of the restaurant, which was illuminated only by a handful of dim lights and candles. With the right company it would have been very romantic. My stomach felt queasy, but I was relieved to have arrived first, so I could breathe and get my bearings. My server, a tall, thin woman named Erin with wavy blonde hair, asked if I wanted anything stronger than water. I confided that some wine might be necessary to take the edge off what would likely be an awkward night. She leaned in to get the scoop. She offered to develop a sign or a code for each scenario—one that would mean things were going well and the other that would mean they weren't.

"Oh, no. There isn't a possibility of needing more time. The goal is to get through dinner as quickly as possible," I explained.

Erin brought me a glass of Chardonnay. I sipped it, hoping Barry would call and say that due to traffic or some work that had suddenly popped up he wouldn't be able to make it.

Then I heard that familiar nasally Borat-meets-Steve-Urkel voice.

"Oh, there she is! Hi, sweetheart," Barry said rather volubly.

Oh, my God! I screamed to myself. He was sporting a thick, black mustache, so thick that it resembled a fake one, and overly gelled hair.

"Hi, Barry. It's nice to see you," I lied and gave him a pat on the back along with a very loose hug, the kind that two grown men offer each other in public.

By that point I had already occupied the table without ordering for a good thirty minutes. As soon as Barry sat down, Erin came to the table to share the specials of the day. She gave a detailed overview of each and every food item for the evening. I broke eye contact with her to glance over at Barry.

"Hello! Hello! What?" Barry screamed into his phone as Erin rattled off the list of specials. "I don't know. I'm at a restaurant now," he screamed into his phone again before awkwardly fumbling with it. "I don't know how to turn this damn thing off," he said.

I bit the insides of my cheeks to stop myself from laughing. This felt like a *Saturday Night Live* skit, but it was just a scene in my life. Erin had finished reciting the specials and was waiting for us to respond.

"Did you get that, Barry?" I asked. "I'm sorry. My friend didn't hear you," I said to Erin, stating the obvious. "Would you mind going over that one more time?"

She repeated the specials and then asked for Barry's drink order. "I don't care what I drink. I'll have whatever she's having," he snapped.

"Um. She's drinking hot water and wine. Is that what you want?"

"Cold water and the same wine as her," he snapped again.

158

Erin delivered Barry's drinks and asked if we were ready to order. Barry leaned completely over his menu with about three inches separating his nose from the surface of the table. He curled up the corner of the menu with one hand and held a candle over it with the other.

"I can't see a damn thing," Barry complained.

I ordered a spinach salad and a bowl of Manhattan clam chowder. Erin coached Barry through his options.

"No problem," she told him after he explained exactly what he wanted. "We'll put the sauce you want on your pasta dish and hold the onions."

"Oh, but I don't want onions," Barry repeated.

"Yes, I understand that. You will not have onions," Erin assured him, and collected our menus. "I'll get you two started with some bread."

"Hey, would you bring us some bread?" Barry asked in a loud voice.

"Yes, I said I would bring you some bread," she explained as politely as she could.

The waitress walked away, and Barry came over to my side of the table. "Hi, sweetheart. We are finally eating dinner together. Isn't that wonderful? It's me," he said, in the same way that someone who had been separated from the love of his life for years might say after a sentimental reunion.

I responded as politely as I could. "Yes, it's nice that we could coordinate our schedules. This is a nice place."

I got up to go to the bathroom, walked around the corner, and burst into laughter when I saw Erin. I couldn't believe this was happening. What was I thinking when I had agreed to have dinner with this strange man? When I returned to my seat, Barry excused himself to use the restroom. He was gone for twenty minutes, long enough for me to text Alex and Katrina a spirited "OMG!" and let them know I was still alive. I learned later that night that during Barry's long absence from my table, he was at the bar in the front of the restaurant treating two other women to drinks.

Barry returned to the table just before our food arrived. Now it was time to make conversation.

"So you're a criminal defense attorney, Barry. What inspired you to pursue that?" I asked.

"Peer pressure," he said shortly.

After I told him what I did, he responded in shock. "What? You wrote a book? You're a reporter? You've traveled? You speak Japanese? What? I had no idea!"

Ironically I had sent him my video pitch for the Oprah Winfrey Network in my shameless attempt to get his vote. In my video I explained that I worked at a women's center, traveled the world, interviewed people, and had a weekend gig as a radio reporter. Barry had told me he had watched my video twenty times. And, of course, the card I had given him when I'd met him mentioned the many professional hats I wore.

"I have the perfect idea for your next book!" Barry blurted. "You could write about the benefits of peer pressure. Look at me," he said. "I'm the man that I am because of peer pressure."

Case in point, I thought. "No, Barry. I'm really not inspired by peer pressure in any way, shape, or form, so that wouldn't be authentic for me to write," I said with a subtle smile. "*You* should write that book, Barry."

I tried to do the math to figure out how old this man was, and after adding up all the years, I estimated him to be forty-six, although my instincts told me to add a few years to that. I asked more questions.

"Have you ever been married, Barry?"

"I don't need to have any experience in that 'cause you and I can get married," he said. "Look what a good couple we make."

I didn't respond.

"When are you going to let me fly you down for dinner?" he asked.

"Never, Barry. That's very kind, but I can't accept a plane ticket from you," I said with a smile.

To quickly change the topic and tap into something Barry might have been familiar with, I asked him his opinion of the Lindsay Lohan case. At the time her name was all over the news for issues related to alcohol, theft, and probation violations.

"Lindsay should have had me as her lawyer. I would have made her stop drinking and gotten her off, and she wouldn't be going to jail right now," Barry said.

"How would she have found you? You don't have a website," I reminded him.

"Word of mouth," Barry coolly responded.

I asked how he would have made Lindsay stop drinking, and he assured me that he was a very persistent man and was good at getting whatever he wanted. I asked him to elaborate.

"Well, I wanted to have dinner with you, and now look what I'm doing," he said.

Damn! He was right about that. Barry slowly pecked away at his noodles, piece by piece. He seemed to be eating extra slowly to prolong our time together.

Then, like a godsend, Erin came back to our table to see if she could get us anything else. I ordered a decaf Americano. Barry suggested I get dessert to go with the coffee.

I glanced at the dessert menu and decided I didn't need any. I let Barry continue to graze on his meal and took another trip to the restroom. When I got around the corner, I ran into Erin again. She suggested that after dinner I stay at the restaurant and hang out with the servers, rather than leave with Barry.

When I got back to the table, Barry insisted that we needed dessert. We agreed on the almost flourless chocolate cake, which we selected because of my gluten allergy.

"Are you sure? That cake might have a little bit of flour in it," the waitress said, trying to spare me from more time with Barry.

"Sure. We'll splurge," I said.

We set the chocolate cake in the center of the table and chiseled at our respective sides for a few minutes. Barry suggested that I extend my stay in Southern California so the two of us could have more time together. I reminded him that in a few days I was scheduled to fly back to Wisconsin to visit my family, so it wouldn't be possible. Barry offered to contact my family and explain that I wouldn't be visiting them because I had agreed to spend more time with Barry. (Yes, he spoke about himself in the third person.)

"No," I said repeatedly with all the politeness I could muster.

"Well, I hope you come to your senses and let me fly you to LA soon. It's kind of hard to go out with a guy from another city without flying over to visit him," he explained.

"Okay, Barry. I'll think that over," I said and started to gather my things, ready to walk out of the restaurant.

"Well, good," he said. "If you'll think about it, that's a success."

I walked out of the restaurant, took three steps with Barry, and then pulled out my cell phone.

"Oh, Barry, I'm so sorry," I said. "My friends just texted me. They're coming here to meet me, so I have to say goodbye now."

I gave him a loose hug and thanked him for dinner. I went back inside and pulled up a seat at the bar in the front section of the restaurant. I burst into laughter along with Erin, the bartender, and the other staff members who had helped me survive my ninety-minute "date."

Katrina and her friend, who had been out to eat at a neighboring restaurant, came to meet me, and we headed back to Katrina's beach house with my decadent leftover chocolate cake in hand. We chatted, giggled, and ended up with a major case of the munchies. Right as we were about to dig into the flourless cake, it fell off the plate and onto the carpet. We stared down at our beautiful chocolate cake that was now covered with dust bunnies. After a pause I quickly picked up the cake and ran to the kitchen to wash off the dust. We lifted our forks in unison and devoured the entire thing. It was the perfect way to end my adventure in Manhattan Beach before heading to Wisconsin to spend time with my family.

CHAPTER SEVENTEEN
Strangers in Transit

I booked a flight out of Los Angeles to Wisconsin via Las Vegas on Southwest Airlines, and I was back on the road, or I should say, in the air, the next day. Southwest is the best airline in the world for people like me—people who are indecisive about travel plans or occasionally miss and need to reschedule flights—because it has no change fees. Passengers are simply assigned an A, B, or C boarding pass when they check in and can sit anywhere they want as long as they board after their respective letter is called. I held a C ticket, which meant that by the time I boarded, mostly middle seats remained.

When I walked onto the plane, there was a friendly redheaded woman in her forties in the aisle seat of row eight. She was chatting with a young blonde woman in an athletic suit who occupied the window seat.

"This seat is open. You can sit with us," the two women offered.

I accepted. I quickly learned that the redhead was a college professor from Arizona in her forties named Jo and had recently married her high school sweetheart and that the blonde woman, Molly, was a twenty-one-year-old college student. Our ages spanned through three decades, but the years that separated us seemed irrelevant. We were simply three women who had a lot in common. Both Molly and Jo agreed to let me interview them.

Molly went first. She had been a basketball player her entire life until a severe injury had taken her off the court. The experience inspired her to think of new possibilities in her life and to consider what she could do to help other people. She now aspired to work with children with disabilities.

"One of the best things you can do in life is to have a positive attitude about all of your experiences," she said. "I think that everything happens for a reason, and that the phrase 'It is what it is' rings true to my life and many others' lives. You will go through ups and downs, and you need to be able to spin those downs to your advantage. I wouldn't have discovered the many opportunities in my life if I hadn't gone through that identity crisis of not being an athlete anymore," Molly explained.

A grumpy man in his sixties sitting in front of us turned around and shushed us several times, but we kept talking quietly. Next I interviewed Jo, who had an interesting take on what had just happened.

"We have three generations of women sitting beside each other. A moment ago I was watching the journalist in her thirties [me] interview the woman in her twenties.

While I was enjoying listening to the experiences and wisdom of the twenty-one-year-old, a man in his sixties continually turned around and told them to be quiet. With so much airplane noise, I honestly didn't think they were that noisy. There might be discomfort with women, particularly young, powerful women. It seemed like yet another attempt to silence women," Jo explained.

"What's the most interesting thing you've learned on this plane ride so far?" I asked her.

"First that age isn't really a big deal with women in terms of goals and what they want to do. It's interesting that even though we're decades apart, I've shared experiences of motivation, independence, and dating. Sitting next to you two women, I thought to myself that the future of womanhood is safe," she replied.

Jo told me about her personal journey that had led her into getting a doctorate in music. Her sister had gotten pregnant as a teenager and her brother had gotten caught up in drugs. She loved music and wanted to do something that would make her parents proud and also pay the bills.

Earlier in the plane ride, Jo had alluded to her relationship with her high school sweetheart. She taught at Arizona State, and her sweetie was a Navy officer based in Chicago. The two maintained their relationship through texting and Skyping and monthly in-person visits. I decided not to let the interview end without prying a little bit.

"When I was in high school, I went to prom with a young man who was also in band," Jo said. "He was a brass player, and I played the clarinet. We ended up going to the same college. We broke up after the first year because we decided we were too young to be in a serious relationship. Our twenty-fifth class reunion came up, and he sent me an e-mail. Two years later I responded. We ended up meeting, feeling as though no time had passed. Now we're married. So, with your first love, you never know what is going to happen."

Jo said that the experience of reuniting with and marrying her very first boyfriend had taught her that maybe young people need to be taken more seriously and given more credit. She couldn't resist closing the interview by offering some advice to other young women trying to figure themselves out.

"It's so important to be true to yourself. Don't rely on men. You need to get educated. You need to get your own job. When you have that sense of independence, you're less likely to be involved in hurtful relationships because you know you can exit and still support yourself. You'll feel more confident. You don't have to stay because of money."

By the time I had finished Jo's interview, the pilot announced that we were approaching our final descent. When we landed at Milwaukee International Airport, the three of us exchanged hugs and headed our separate directions. I never saw or heard from these women again, but I relished the fact that wherever I went, strangers that were equally inspirational awaited me. No matter how far I traveled on my own, I would never be alone.

CHAPTER EIGHTEEN
Back to the Roots

The next afternoon my sister, my six-month-old niece, and I finally arrived at my parents' home in Whitehall, Wisconsin. Ava had grown to a nineteen-pound baby. The first time I'd met her, when she was just a few months old, she mostly cried and slept. Now she had developed her own little personality. She laughed, turned her head, reached for toys, screamed when she wanted something, tugged on my dangly earrings, grabbed a handful of my long hair and pulled it, or grabbed my fingers and stuffed them into her mouth.

Our town was small, and we always planned ahead for some exciting activities. On Wednesdays, for example, the portable Chinese restaurant rolled into the hardware store parking lot so locals could get takeout orders. On Wednesday morning, my aunt and uncle, who lived four blocks away, popped over for a surprise visit. We sat in the living room chatting as my sister breastfed her baby. Then we passed around the menu for the restaurant on wheels.

My dad and I drove to the hardware store parking lot. One man worked at the counter, and dozens of customers drove into the lot—nurses on break, men from the factory with slightly greasy hair, grandmothers, young families, bankers, and people from neighboring towns. I sprinted to the counter to put in my family's order.

"Can I help . . . ?" the young Chinese man began to ask, and then his phone rang. "Just one moment," he said.

"Okay, anything else?" he asked the caller, as if he were ready to wrap up the order. She presumably said yes dozens of times. He kept flipping the page of his green order book.

"Okay, anything else?"

It went on and on. I finally ordered and then moved off to the side to wait for our food. My dad parked his gray Pontiac and joined me. He was particularly sharp that day. The combination of his mental health condition and all the medication he took often caused him to be fuzzy, tired, or slightly out of sorts. On this day he was focused, present in the conversation, and incredibly charming. A woman from town recognized him, and the two of them chatted. Thirty minutes later we were on our way home with six take-out Chinese meals.

We brought our meals out to the front deck of my parents' home and set up the table. Ava jumped up and down in her bouncy chair and played with toys while the rest of us took turns eating and running into the house to get an extra item—like ketchup (for some reason, a family staple, even for Chinese food), soy sauce, milk, corn on the cob, fruit, dessert, and coffee.

Something weird was about to happen with the weather. The sky was half sunny and half gray. Within the past hour, it had cooled down from a humid ninety degrees to around seventy degrees.

Suddenly rain started to come down, so we packed up everything and moved into the house. Ten minutes later the storm passed and the sun was back out. My aunt was on baby duty that afternoon so my sister could take a break. My uncle bolted back to the comfort of his home, and my mom and I headed to the local Amish grocery store so we could pick up our seasonal shipment of cherries.

In our small city, outside the grocery store and other shops, there were hitching posts for the horses and buggies that the Amish drove to town while running errands. It was customary to slow down or move slightly to the center of the road to avoid hitting a buggy. An Amish woman helped my mom with house cleaning each month. An Amish family had built Ava's crib. Although I loved fashion way too much to ever consider wearing a bonnet on my head or a drab dress underneath a plain apron, there was something very intriguing about living a life of such humility and simplicity. I loved that this was the place I came from. It kept life in perspective, and in some ways it felt more exotic than whatever foreign city I would have found myself in that summer had I not used every penny in my bank account to chase my dream of getting my own show on the Oprah Winfrey Network.

My mom and I returned home from the Amish grocery store and carried in our ten pounds of cherries. The sky had shifted once again, and the weather seemed to be taking another turn. Ava was screaming up a storm. She wanted her mom. No one else would do. We moved into the house, and minutes later sheets of rain pounded down. Then the tornado siren went off. I grabbed my laptop and a *Chicken*

Soup for the Soul board game and headed for the basement, along with the whole family. Ava drifted off to sleep after receiving a small dose of my sister's breast milk. I set up a card table and put it over little Ava's car seat, so that in the off chance a tornado struck or something collapsed, she would have an extra shield.

I sat in a rocking chair, my mom and dad squeezed into a love seat, and my sister cuddled up with a pillow so she could chat and keep an eye on her baby. I pulled out the first question in the *Chicken Soup for the Soul* game. I can't remember exactly what the question was, but it prompted my dad to open up.

As the middle child, he shared that he had felt like the forgotten member of his family. He had worked long, grueling hours on his childhood farm. He wanted something more for himself, and at the time the only way to tap into more was to join the Army. He worked on the farm up until an hour before he had to catch the train to go to boot camp. He only received one package during his six months of active duty. His mom, my grandma, sent him a package of cookies and a note saying how much she missed him. My dad spent a total of eight years as a member of the Army Reserves. He had an opportunity to become a male nurse, but turned it down because he didn't want anyone to call him a sissy.

My heart sank as he confided this to my family. I realized that the rocky relationship I'd had with my dad when I was a child was part of what had inspired me to leave and travel. I wished for a second that I could turn back time and give my dad some of my resiliency. I had spent much of my adult life advocating for my dad. I always sensed that he felt ashamed of who he was. I dreamt of doing something great in my lifetime with my dad's last name still attached to mine, so I could make him proud.

Even though my dad and I had experienced our share of struggles over the years, we were the spitting image of each other, from our deep-set eyes to our facial structure. I imagine that when he saw me, he saw himself—everything he loved and aspired to be and everything he hated or struggled to accept.

On Sunday night my dad helped me make dinner. He chopped olives, onions, lettuce, and tomatoes. I prepared quinoa and a mixture that would result in a delicious Greek salad. We paired this with baked vegetables and a meat dish that my mom made for all the meat eaters in the family. We brought our meal to the front deck and began to eat. At seven p.m. the sun still shone brightly, so brightly that we had to cup our hands over our eyes to see one another. We finished our meals, and no one raced away from the table. We sat there reminiscing. My dad clearly had been sparked to think about memories he had filed away deep in his soul after our night of bonding. He wanted to talk more. We couldn't stop him, and we didn't want to. I went into my house to get my recording device so I could preserve his story.

My dad told us how he had met my mom, how he had courted her, and how they had ended up sleeping in a car in Wisconsin Dells, Wisconsin for their honeymoon. We talked about the Army again and the sad fact that he had passed up his chance to become a nurse. At one point he stopped and told us why he thought it was all worth it.

"Honey, it would have been a really good life if I had been a nurse, and I would be retired by now, but it wasn't supposed to work out," he explained.

"Why's that, Dad?" I asked.

"If I was a nurse, I wouldn't have met Mom, and I wouldn't have the two of you girls."

We sat outside until the bright sun started to hide behind the hills and the yellow sky faded into a soft gray, signifying that the day was coming to an end.

I had interviewed people practically every day since I had turned twenty. Finally I heard the story I had been waiting for—the story of my dad. I had traveled the entire world and shamelessly chased a dream around the country, only to be led back to the spot where my journey had begun. This isn't where my journey ends, but it will always be a stopover point, a safe place to land, and my home. There was no shortcut I could have taken to arrive here, or any step I could have skipped to find myself here. Everything happened exactly as it was meant to.

Life is imperfect, incredibly messy, amazing, and tragic all at the same time. It's natural that it won't go according to plans or that in hindsight we'll always think of something we could or should have done differently. But it's the decisions that we made or didn't make that led us to the wonderful spot we are in right now. From here we can decide which course of action to take. We can hold on to regrets about what we did or didn't do, or we can embrace the experiences we've accumulated along the way as life content. I choose the latter.

About the Author

Sharon K. Sobotta is a journalist, an educator, and a world traveler. At the age of seventeen, she was the recipient of a Kikkoman soy sauce scholarship, which sent her from rural Wisconsin to Tokyo, Japan. Since then, Sharon has been a lifelong globetrotter—volunteering, interviewing people, living alongside locals, and taking up temporary roots wherever she goes.

Sharon continually takes the road less traveled to capture the stories of people from all walks of life—stories that run the gamut from the familiar to the unexpected. From the everyday struggles that men and women experience with relationships and love, to the societal impact of xenophobia, Islamophobia, racism, and sexism, there is no issue Sharon is unwilling to tackle. As a field reporter for Pacifica and FSRN Radio, Sharon has been on the ground covering stories ranging from the Occupy movement in Oakland, California, to the impact of globalization in Ubud, Bali, Indonesia.

When Sharon is not traveling, reporting or writing, she serves as the director of the Women's Resource Center at St. Mary's College of California, where she strives to inspire people to imagine a world that is equitable and violence free. Sharon resides in the San Francisco Bay Area with her significant other, Hector, and their daughter Esperanza.

15278458R10102

Made in the USA
Charleston, SC
26 October 2012